ALL THE DAYS

DAILY DEVOTIONS FOR BUSY BELIEVERS

by
Jerry Vines

All the Days: Daily Devotions for Busy Believers
by Jerry Vines

Copyright © 2012 by Jerry Vines

ISBN 978-0-9826561-8-1

Printed in the United States of America by Lightning Source, Inc.

Unless otherwise indicated, all Scripture taken from the King James Version of the Holy Bible.

Cover design by Jessica Anglea www.jessicaanglea.com
Text design by Debbie Patrick, Vision Run, www.visionrun.com

Free Church Press
P.O. Box 1075
Carrollton, GA 30112

Dedication

To my wife, Janet, who has been the love of my life and my faithful companion these 50+ years. I have watched her grow in her Christian life as she has faithfully read her Bible and prayed "All The Days."

Contents

Preface

Early in my Christian life I discovered the importance of daily devotions. Christians need a daily time when they read their Bible, letting God talk to them. Then, they pray, talking to God.

My primary devotional reading has been the Bible, of course. But, I have found it helpful to also read devotional books. I have been blessed through the years by devotionals written by Spurgeon, Chambers, Cowan, King and many more.

For many years I have wanted to put together a devotional book. My desire has now come to fruition. The intention of this daily devotion entitled *All the Days* is to help you get something from God's Word everyday and suggest a brief prayer. Hopefully, this devotional book will be helpful to you.

Just a word about the format. Each month begins with a summary page about the Bible book(s) for that month. I move from Old Testament to New Testament books each month. Each day there is a brief statement from some verse in that particular day's location. And, if time permits, I also include a chapter that you might read. Also, I include some alliterated outlines to assist you in your reading.

My prayer is that these devotions will help you, as God speaks to you (Bible reading) and you speak to God (prayer) "all the days"(Psalm 23:6) of this year!

Jerry Vines

January

BEGINNINGS.

*Genesis means beginnings.
As we start a new year it is
appropriate that we begin
our year with Genesis!*

JANUARY 1

READING: Genesis 1

"In the beginning God ..." Genesis 1:1

That's the only way to start a universe, a Bible, a year, a marriage or a happy life! Genesis 1 opens the door to the beginnings of things. The special emphasis here is upon God's creation of the universe. It is stated in beautiful, accurate statements. Note that the creation days are parallel. Days one through three tell about God FORMING the world. Days four through six tell us about God FILLING the world. And it all starts with God! As you read this opening chapter of the Bible and the creation is revealed, it becomes obvious that the account is building to a climax. And that is? On day six God creates man! Scientists have come to understand the anthropic principle. It is now recognized that the whole creation was specially designed for people! What a beginning!

PRAYER: *"Dear Lord, thank You for creating me. And thank You for creating a world just for me."*

JANUARY 2

READING: Genesis 2

"And the Lord God formed man of the dust of the ground ..." Genesis 2:7

A contradictory account to the creation account in Genesis 1? No. They are complementary. Often writers in early days used what is known as the law of recurrence. That is, they would give a general account of a subject, then would go over the same ground again, filling in the details. It's kind of like an artist painting. First, the broad strokes will be made. Then, the details will be filled in. The creation account in Genesis 1 is chronological and general in nature. Genesis 2's account is thematic in nature. Thus, man is mentioned before animals. Man is the center of the picture! And, a new name for God is given. In Genesis 1 God is revealed as *Elohim*—His CREATIVE name. In Genesis 2 He is revealed as *Jehovah*—His REDEMPTIVE name! This anticipates the sad reality of Genesis 3. God is our Creator. We also need Him as our Redeemer.

PRAYER: *"O Lord, You not only created me. You can also redeem me!"*

JANUARY 3

"Adam ... where art thou?" Genesis 3:9

READING: Genesis 3

Reality TV is very popular these days. Very often the real lives of people are very tumultuous and troubled. Genesis 3 is real life as well. It gives the sad, very real account of the entrance of sin into the world and the tragic fall of man. This is not a fairy tale. Romans 5:12 makes it very clear that this is actual history. SATAN. Lurking in the Garden of Eden was the old gate-crasher, Satan, appearing as the Serpent. The account of how Satan caused the fall of Adam and Eve is as old as the garden of Eden, but as new as how people fall into sin daily. SIN. Eve falls. Adam falls. SEARCHING. Then, God comes walking in the garden, asking this question: "Where art thou?" What is our answer to this probing question today?

PRAYER: *"Lord, thank You for providing the precious blood of Your Son to make possible our clothing of salvation."*

JANUARY 4

READING: Genesis 4

"... a fugitive and a vagabond shalt thou be in the earth" Genesis 4:12

Genesis 3 shows the root of sin. Genesis 4 shows the fruit of sin. The tragic account of Cain's murder of Abel brought sin's horror to Adam and Eve in a most poignant manner. The chapter is built around Cain. He is mentioned 13 times. 1 John 3:12 speaks of "the way of Cain." We see his CORRUPTION, his CONVICTION and his CONCLUSION. Sin turned Cain and people today into fugitives, running from home; and vagabonds, having no home. Christ turns us into "strangers," away from home and "pilgrims," on the way home (1 Peter 2:11)! Cain's line drops off the page. Between 4:24 and 4:25 it seems the countdown to judgment is on: 5-4-3-2-1-0. Silence. Then water pouring and the shrieks of condemned people. And the washing of water against a saving ark!

PRAYER: *"Lord Jesus, I thank You that You have given me a better home than this one!"*

JANUARY 5

READING: Genesis 5

> *"And Enoch walked with God: and he was not; for God took him."*
> *Genesis 5:24*

Genesis 5 has been called the death chapter in the Bible. The phrase "and he died" is found 8 times. It's like the solemn tolling of a funeral bell; the squeaking wheels of a funeral carriage; the dropping of dirt clods on a grave. It is a vindication of God's Word. God said, "lest ye die." Satan said, "Ye shall not surely die." "and he died ... and he died." New Testament truth is illustratrated. I Corinthians 15:22 says, "in Adam all die; in Christ all are made alive." But, in this dark death chapter there is a burst of light. Enoch lived; but he didn't die. He walked with God and God translated him to heaven! Walking with God carries the idea of walking IN: That's JUSTIFICATION; walking ON: That's SANCTIFICATION; walking OUT: That's GLORIFICATION!

PRAYER: *"Heavenly Father, help me to walk with You today to experience a little bit of heaven on earth."*

JANUARY 6

READING: Genesis 7

> *"Come thou, and all thy house into the ark"* Genesis 7:1

Genesis 1-11 gives us HUMAN history. The beginnings of human history are presented around 4 historical events: creation; the fall; the flood; and the tower of Babel. Today we look at the flood. The chapter shows us Satan's PERVERSION on the earth, Noah's PERFECTION on the earth, and God's PROVISION on the earth. The wickedness of the earth is awful to behold. The "sons of God" who married the "daughters of men" may refer to an unspeakable spiritual perversion or a reference to a union of the godly line of Seth with the ungodly line of Cain. Either way, the result is unspeakable corruption. But, a lily may grow in a cesspool. Noah "found grace" (v. 8). God provided a way for Noah and his family. An ark. God invites, "Come into the ark ... " God's invitation is, "Whosoever will, come."

PRAYER: *"Thank You, Lord Jesus, for being my Ark of salvation."*

JANUARY 7

READING: Genesis 8-9

" ... that the bow may be seen in the cloud." Genesis 9:14

How beautiful is a rainbow. Rainbows appear when sunlight goes through water in the air. Each drop becomes a prism showing the colors hidden in the white light of the sun. Rainbows have meaning. God says it is a TOKEN (v. 12). It points to many of the attributes of God. We learn from the flood about His severity. From the (rain)bow we learn of His goodness, kindness and faithfulness. A bow is also a TESTIMONY (v.14). Clouds inevitably come in life, but there is a bow in every cloud. Going through a storm? Look for the bow of God's promises. A bow is also a TYPE. There are striking parallels between the bow and the cross. From the darkness of Calvary shines the multi-faceted love of God. This word is also used for a battle bow. From the cloud comes the bow. The battle is over!

PRAYER: "Thank You, Lord, for putting a rainbow in my clouds."

JANUARY 8

READING: Genesis 11

"Let us ... Let us ... "Genesis 11:3, 7

There are four major historical events in Genesis 1-11. The creation tells us where we came from. The fall explains why we are like we are. The flood/ark tells us God's attitude toward sin and the sinner. Now, the tower of Babel shows us where civilization is headed. We get a glimpse into the RULER (10:8-10), REBELLION (11:1-4), and RUIN (11:5-9) of godless culture. The prime mover seems to be Nimrod. His name means, to rebel. He is first in the godless line of earthly dictators. His ambition is to establish world empire. Man in rebellion to God seeks to build a tower. Three times they say, "Let us." Rebellion to God says, "Let us." Submission says, "Thy will be done." So God says, "Let us." Trinity collaborates and man's culture lies in ruins. Man's culture only produces confusion.

PRAYER: "O God, You always have Your way in the end. And I am glad."

JANUARY 9

"So Abram departed, as the Lord had spoken to him ..." Genesis 12:4

READING: Genesis 12:1-8

Genesis 1-11 gives us the history of the HUMAN race. Genesis 12 begins the history of the HEBREW race. Four great men are featured: Abraham, Isaiah, Jacob and Joseph. Abraham! He is called the friend of God and the father of the faithful. He gives us a great example of what it means to trust the Lord and make our journey of life a journey of faith (Hebrews 11:8-10). LOSTNESS. His story begins in Ur of the Chaldees (modern Iraq). He is a successful 75-year-old businessman. BLESSEDNESS. Then God steps in. He offers a different kind of life and a better home. God calls. Promising seven blessings for one act of obedience (vv. 1-2). When we say, "I will," God says, "I will." Seven times! Who knows what God will do with you, if you will heed the call of faith.

PRAYER: "Lead me, Lord, and I will follow."

JANUARY 10

READING: Genesis 12:9-13:4

" ... where his tent had been ... unto the place of the altar ..."

Genesis 13:3-4

Abraham stumbled on his journey of faith. We do too! The Bible doesn't encourage us to stumble; but it does encourage us when we stumble. We see here faith RECEDING (12:10) and faith RETURNING (13:3-4). Because of a famine in the land Abraham took a detour down to Egypt (12:10ff). Famines do come. Unexpected problems. Disappointments. Famines test our faith. Worst possible move? Hightailing it to Egypt! This world will give you nothing but heartache. Better to starve in Canaan than to live in luxury in Egypt. The story isn't pleasant. Abram becomes a liar and deceiver. He risks his own wife. He is rebuked by a pagan king. So what is the cure? He built a tent (separation) and an altar (devotion) while in Canaan. None is mentioned while he is down in Egypt. He returns to his tent and altar!

PRAYER: "Heavenly Father, I have often stumbled. Thank You for the road back."

JANUARY 11

READING: Genesis 13-14, 19

> *"... and pitched his tent toward Sodom." Genesis 13:12*

Judge Robert Bork wrote a book entitled, *Slouching Toward Sodom*. It draws from the sad experience of Lot, Abram's nephew. BELIEVER. Hard to believe, but Lot was a believer (See Luke 17:28-29; 2 Peter 2:7-8). BACKSLIDDER. He is the classic picture in the Bible of a believer who lives for time, not eternity; a saved soul, but a lost life. He barely made it through a corridor of fire to safety (see 1 Corinthians 3:13-15). The slow, sad decline of Lot is recorded in a series of verses. He pitched his tent toward Sodom (Genesis 13:12); he dwelt in Sodom (Genesis 14:12); he was the mayor of Sodom (Genesis 19:1). And, it all started because he pitched his life in a questionable direction. What a tragedy: he started out LOOKING FOR A CITY; he wound up LIVING IN A CAVE.

PRAYER: *"Heavenly Father, help me to maintain Biblical separation (tent) and communion (altar)."*

JANUARY 12

READING: Genesis 16

> *"... go in unto my maid; it may be that I may obtain children by her."*
> *Genesis 16:2*

Abraham stumbled more than one time. So do we. PROMISE. God had promised Abraham his seed would be as numerous as the stars (Read Genesis 15:1-6). God fulfilled the promise. PRESUMPTION. But Abraham ran ahead. His and Sarah's biological clocks are ticking. He has God's Word; he doesn't have patience. Thus the sad account of a child by his wife's handmaid, an Egyptian named Hagar. A painful detour indeed. Most of us don't like to wait. We like standing on the promises; we aren't so thrilled to wait for the promises! When the promises don't come according to our schedule we want to do something. The flesh always wants to help God keep His promises. Ishmael is born. O the heartache the Ishmael's of our lives cause. We need to read again Hebrews 10:36.

PRAYER: *"Help me, Lord, to wait on You and not run ahead of You."*

JANUARY 13

READING: Genesis 18

"... *I will not destroy it for ten's sake.*" *Genesis 18:32*

Judgment clouds are gathering over Sodom. It's just a matter of time. PROMISE. Thee men appear at Abraham's house. They are, of course, more than men (See Hebrews 13:2). Abraham realizes that one of them is the Lord of glory. This is what is called a theophany—a pre-incarnate revelation in the Old Testament of the Lord Jesus Christ. The promise of God that Sarah will bear Abraham a son is reiterated. But, also the solemn message of Sodom's judgment is delivered (Genesis 18:20-22). PRAYER. Then Abraham begins to plead for Sodom. His nephew, Lot, is living there. We have no indication Abraham ever even visited Sodom. It's good for believers to stay out of Sodom! He begins to intercede for the godless city. Who comes closest to winning sinners? Not the "Lots" of the faith, but the "Abrahams" pleading for their salvation.

PRAYER: "Help me, dear Savior, to pray for sinners to be saved."

JANUARY 14

READING: Genesis 20

"... *She is my sister ...* " *Genesis 20:2*

Haven't we heard that before? Indeed, we have. Ever repeated a sin you thought you had conquered? Probably most of us have. Abraham did. He had lied about his wife before unbelievers way back in Genesis 12:10-20. Surely he repented. But, it pops up again. In verse 1-8 we see the RECURRENCE of this OLD SIN. Then, we learn about the REPETITION of an OLD SHAME (vv. 9-16). But, praise God, vv. 17-18 teach about the RELIEF of an OLD SOLUTION! I think Abraham somewhere found a place of prayer, faced this old sin, confessed it and committed himself anew to the Lord. Praise God, so can we! One of the best worn verses in my Bible is 1 John 1:9. This is no enticement to commit an old sin, but a promise to claim cleansing.

PRAYER: "Lord, here I am again. Confessing an old sin. And claiming 1 John 1:9."

JANUARY 15

READING: Genesis 21

"Cast out this woman and her son ..." Genesis 21:10

The long awaited promise has arrived! Isaac is born. OBSTRUCTION. But, Ishmael is there also. What about him? Ishmael stands between Abraham and total commitment. Is there an "Ishmael" in your life? Some friend or material possession or habit or point of personal pride? Whatever the "Ishmael" in your life, God can't use you to the fullest until as long as it hinders. God's word is sometimes painful. "Cast out ... " This is not easy. It's not pleasant, but painful. When the knife cuts, the vine bleeds. When the dross is consumed, the fire is hot. OBEDIENCE. But, "early in the morning" (v. 14) Abraham obeys. As Genesis 21 closes (v. 33) Abraham is by a well of water, talking to the Lord. Total commitment is the happy, helpful and holy way. Is there some "Ishmael" in your life today?

PRAYER: *"Heavenly Father, take away the "Ishmael" in my life that I might be totally dedicated to You."*

JANUARY 16

READING: Genesis 22

"Take now thine only son Isaac ... and offer him there ..." Genesis 22:2

Someone said, "A faith that can't be TESTED can't be TRUSTED." Abraham is facing the greatest test of his life. He has lost Ishmael. But, he still has Isaac. Then comes the STUNNING ORDER— offer up your beloved son, Isaac. Put yourself in his place. This must have crushed Abraham's world. The bottom falls out; the roof caves in; the walls crumble. His response? The SIMPLE OBEDIENCE— "early in the morning."(v. 3). Obedience is often painful. And often perplexing. Isaac's question is significant: "Where is the Lamb?" Centuries later John the Baptist pointed to Jesus and said, "Behold the Lamb ..." (John 1:29). Abraham raises the knife. God intervenes and says, "now I know ..." (v. 12). God provides the SUBSTITUTE OFFERING— a thorn-crowned ram! God takes the "Ishmaels" from our life to return them no more. He takes our "Isaacs" only to return them to us forever!

PRAYER: *"O Lord, today I lay my all on the altar."*

JANUARY 17

READING: Genesis 23

> *"And Abraham came to mourn for Sarah and to weep for her."*
> Genesis 23:2

The B's of aging: baldness, bifocals and bunions! And a sadder one—burials. His beloved wife Sarah dies. Look at his TEARS (v. 2). Her death meant gladness for her, but sadness for him. The old white-haired man stoops over her cold, lifeless form and tears flow unhindered. There is a loveliness to tears, and some lessons. But also, thank God for the LORD of tears. God will one day wipe away our tears. Look at his TESTIMONY (vv. 3-4). We can have a testimony when we lose loved ones. But, don't fail to look at his TRUST (vv. 7-20). Sarah is buried in the Promised Land. Abraham trusts God for the promise of the land. When loved ones die, claim the promises of resurrection!

PRAYER: *"Lord, if I face the death of loved ones, help me to trust You to one day dry my tears and keep all Your promises to me."*

JANUARY 18

READING: Genesis 24

> *"Wilt thou go ... I will go."* Genesis 24:58

Isaac needs a wife. This lengthy chapter tells how he got one. SEEKING. Abraham's servant goes to the homeland to seek Isaac's bride. Just so God is seeking a bride (the church) for His Son. With 10 camels loaded down with his master's riches he heads out. The servant finds Rebekah. After a several days the servant tells the story of his master and extends the invitation to Rebekah to love one she had not seen (See 1 Peter 1:8). RESPONDING. She said, "I will go!" The sovereign God invites us to come to Christ by our choice. She took the long journey to Isaac. When she saw him (v. 64) she dismounted the camel and went to him! One day we will leave this world and go to meet our Heavenly Bridegroom!

PRAYER: *"Lord, thank You for inviting me to be a part of the Bride of Christ. I look forward to seeing the One I have not seen, but love."*

JANUARY 19

READING: Genesis 27

"... I shall seem to him a deceiver ..." Genesis 27:12

Isaac was caught between his dad and a son. The ordinary son of a great father (Abraham); and the ordinary father of a great son (Jacob). The story of his FAMILY (Genesis 25) and his ACTIVITY (Genesis 26) and especially his TRAGEDY (Genesis 27) can help us today. Isaac and Rebekah have 2 sons—Esau and Jacob. Same parents; same birthday; same advantages. Yet, Esau moves away from the things of God and Jacob moves toward them. Isaac's home life is sadly typical of some today. There is DECEPTION (Genesis 27:1-40) and DISRUPTION (Genesis 27:41-46). Jacob deceives his dad. Esau threatens to kill his twin brother. Rebekah sends Jacob away "for a few days" (v. 44). She never saw him again. There can be a brighter picture. God can help families.

PRAYER: *"Heavenly Father, help us with our family issues."*

JANUARY 20

READING: Genesis 28

"Surely the Lord is in this place; and I knew it not." Genesis 28:16

Jacob now occupies the center of the Genesis stage. We identify easily with Jacob, so human. We focus today on his experience at Bethel. Picture Jacob LEAVING his home (vv. 10-11). A boy with problems: conflict at home. Fear of his brother. Running for his life. Not unlike many young people today. His first night from home is at dreary Bethel, trying to sleep with a stone for a pillow. Then, God reveals a LADDER! (v. 12). Someone else is at Bethel! Angels are ascending and descending upon it. What a picture of Jesus! (See John 1:51). The answer to Jacob's problems, and ours, is Jesus. He meets the LORD (vv. 13-15). The result? DEDICATION (vv. 16-22) and CONSECRATION (vv. 18-22). All of us need a Bethel, a place to meet the Lord in dedication and consecration.

PRAYER: *"Help my devotional time today to be my Bethel."*

JANUARY 21

READING: Genesis 29-31

> *"Thus have I been twenty years in thy house ..." Genesis 31:41*

Those were the words of Jacob as he exploded on Uncle Laban. SALVATION. When Jacob left Bethel (27:1) he was on the mountain top. He was saved! SANCTIFICATION. But, it's one thing to be saved; it's quite another to be sanctified. Conversion is an event; sanctification is a process. Jacob is going to live with Laban in Haran, he thinks. He's really enrolling in the School of Hard Knocks. At Bethel Jacob learns what God is like; at Haran he learns what people are like. A tough lesson indeed. In Laban he meets his match. For 20 years he works for a man more cunning and deceitful than himself. It's like God makes Laban a mirror and says, "Here's what you are like, Jacob." Will you see yourself in other people today?

PRAYER: *"Lord, I know You are working to make me like Christ. Help me to allow You to change me."*

JANUARY 22

READING: Genesis 32

> *" ... and there wrestled a man with him until the breaking of the day."*
> *Genesis 32:24.*

A crisis experience may cause us to yield to God. Jacob had such an experience. He is running from uncle Laban and into brother Esau! Now he is at the ford Jabbok alone. Suddenly a hand seizes him! He isn't looking for a fight. He's trying to hold on! The Wrestler is none other than the Lord (See Hosea 12:4-5). All he can do is cling. And cling he does until the blessing comes. God's question exposes him—"What is thy name?" (v. 27). He meets the Lord and he sees himself. "Jacob," he answered. Just a cheat and a liar. God gives him a new name—"Israel," a prince with God and men. When the day dawns he is a BROKEN man (v. 31), but also a BLESSED (vv. 26-30) and a BRANDED (vv. 31-32) man!

PRAYER: *"Lord, help me to learn that by my limp I live."*

19

JANUARY 23

READING: Genesis 35

> *"... Arise, go up to Bethel, ... and make there an altar unto God ..."*
> *Genesis 35:1*

We sometimes think a deeper experience with the Lord will solve all our problems. Not! Jacob had such an experience at Jabbok, but he still has his sorrows and heartaches. So do we. The good news is, when we fail, the Lord calls us back to Himself. RETURN. Back to Bethel! Is there a word, just mentioned, that will take you back to a place of sacred, fragrant memories? Some place of sweet spiritual experience? Where is your "Bethel?" REVELATION. When Jacob gets back to Bethel he calls it *El-Bethel*, which means, the mighty God of the house of God. Jacob has come to a greater understanding. God is now more important to Him than any place. The hymn writer expressed it — "Once earthly joy I craved; sought peace and rest; Now, Thee alone I seek, give what is best."

PRAYER: *"Dear Lord, may I turn my Bethels into El-Bethels."*

JANUARY 24

READING: Genesis 37

> *"... Behold, this dreamer cometh." Genesis 37:19*

Joseph takes up one-fourth of Genesis. God creating the stars takes up only five words (1:16). God is more interested in PEOPLE than PLANETS. He's more about making SAINTS than STARS! Joseph's life is filled with helpful lessons for us. We are told about his FAMILY (vv. 1-4). Joseph is his dad's favorite. It didn't make him popular with his brothers. We are also told about his FUTURE (vv. 5-11). God revealed the future to Joseph in some dreams. His brothers didn't like that either. So, we are told about his FATE (vv. 12ff). When Joseph came looking for his brothers they tagged him with their derisive title, "The dreamer." There are some people you will encounter who don't want to make anything of their life and they will try to keep you from dreaming big dreams for yours.

PRAYER: *"Help me, Heavenly Father, to dream special dreams of living for You."*

JANUARY 25

READING: Genesis 39

"And the Lord was with Joseph" Genesis 39:2

Sometimes the Bible sums up a life in one sentence. For Joseph it is the phrase, "The Lord was with Joseph." It occurs four times in Genesis 39. The New Testament picks it up when it summarizes Joseph's life (See Acts 7:9). We see that the Lord was with Joseph in his VOCATION (vv. 1-6). Now in Egypt he wears the servant's garb in Potiphar's house. The Lord is with us in our work. He was with him in his TEMPTATION (vv. 7-18). He refused the advances of Potiphar's wife. When we are tempted the Lord will help us. And, God was with him in his INCARCERATION (vv.19-23). Do right and it will come out right. Right? Wrong! Not always. But, the Lord is with us and has a plan through all our trials. Remember today, the Lord is with you.

PRAYER: *"Thank You, Lord, that You are always with me."*

JANUARY 26

READING: Genesis 40-41

"Then Pharoah sent and called Joseph ..." Genesis 41:14

Prison doors slam behind Joseph and Satan whispers, "Now what about your God?" Joseph perhaps spent ten years in prison for a crime he didn't commit. God gives unusual tests. We give the lesson, then the test. God gives the tests, then the lessons! He is tested as the FAITHFUL servant (40:1-3). He does his best in prison. And he is faithful to tell the truth to Pharoah's butler and baker. He is then tested as the FORGOTTEN servant (40:14-41:13). He asks to be remembered, but he is forgotten. Does ingratitude ever bother you? Ah, but he becomes the FAVORED servant (41:14-57). In rapid succession events transpire to take Joseph from prisoner to Prime Minister! And Joseph honors the Lord before Pharoah (41:15-16). Let us honor Him in all our tests today.

PRAYER: *"Thank You, Lord, You are working in ways I do not know."*

JANUARY 27

READING: Genesis 42

" ... we are verily guilty concerning our brother ..." Genesis 42:21

Has God forgotten about Joseph's brothers' sin against Joseph? What about "be sure your sin will find you out?" (Numbers 32:23). "The wheels of God's judgment grind slowly, but surely." Here is a classic study on the conscience, that inner judge that condemns us when we do wrong. For a while they had an ABANDONED conscience. There is no evidence theirs bothered them. But, standing before Joseph they exhibit an AWAKENED conscience. God uses a series of events to arouse their guilt. Famine in the land—Is Joseph yet alive in Egypt? Journey to Egypt— Is one of those slaves in the field Joseph? Audience with Joseph— his ultimatum to bring Benjamin back stirs them indeed. When they see the money in the sack their conscience is ALARMED. Their conscience found them. But in a wonderful place—in the presence of Joseph!

PRAYER: "Lord Jesus, may I find peace for my conscience in Your presence."

JANUARY 28

READING: Genesis 43-45

" ... it was not you that sent me hither, but God ..." Genesis 45:8

BITTERNESS. Many people are filled with bitterness. Life has dealt them unkind blows and they are determined to go through life miserable and making others miserable. If anyone ever had a right to be bitter, it was Joseph Sold by his brothers into a strange land; he did right and went to prison for it; forgotten and neglected. His brothers stand before him. As his brothers stand before him he makes himself known. Now's the time, Joseph Pour it all out. BLESSEDNESS. But, he shows not one trace of bitterness. Why? He mentions God four times (Genesis 45: 5, 7-8). We get bitter because we fail to see God's hand in our life. "My Father's ways may twist and turn, My heart may throb and ache, But in my soul I'm glad to know He maketh no mistake."

PRAYER: "Lord, I lay down my bitterness at the foot of the cross, where You prayed, 'Father, forgive them ... '"

JANUARY 29

READING: Genesis 48

> *" ... Israel strengthened himself, and sat upon the bed." Genesis 48:2*

Do you have dying grace? No? You aren't dying yet! God promises His children grace for every juncture of life (See 2 Corinthians 12:9). Jacob (Israel) is coming to the close of his life. Hebrews 11:21 mentions the faith of Jacob in connection with his death. Evidently the finest thing about his life was the close of it. Jacob is not afraid as he faces death. Why? God's gift of dying grace. Jacob has his LORD (48:3-4). The name of the Lord is upon his lips. He has his LOVED ONES (48:8ff). His children and grandchildren were the joy and delight of his heart. Special to know at death there will be loved ones there. He has his LEGACY. Facing chilly Jordan he leaves his family with a testimony and a treasure (48:20-22).

PRAYER: "Dear Lord, thank You that at death You will give me dying grace."

JANUARY 30

READING: Genesis 49

> *" ... until Shiloh come ..." Genesis 49:10*

Jacob is dying. His 12 sons solemnly file in. His words to each son reveal character and constitute a remarkable prophecy about the destiny of each family. In the midst of these words there is a promise about the coming Messiah, our Savior, the Lord Jesus Christ. In this prophecy we see the SOVEREIGNTY of Jesus (49:10). When Judah (Israel) loses the power to govern itself, then Messiah would come. Christ was born; Rome ruled . We see the SWEETNESS of Jesus (49:20). Jesus was born in Bethlehem, the house of bread. He feeds the hungry heart. We see the SERVICE of Jesus (49:21). A "Hind let loose," — His daily walk. "Goodly words" — His daily talk. We see the SUFFERING of Jesus (vv. 23-24). O how Jesus suffered! Jacob closes his eyes in death; he opens them in heaven!

PRAYER: "Thank You, dear Father, that You sent your Son just like you said You would."

JANUARY 31

READING: Genesis 50

" ... and he was put in a coffin in Egypt." Genesis 50:26

Genesis starts with a creation; it ends with a coffin. It begins with glory; its ends with a grave. It begins with a living God; it ends with a dead man. Mankind has two problems— sin and death (See Romans 5:12). The chapter begins with the FUNERAL of Jacob (vv.1-13), continues with the FEAR of the brothers (vv.14-21) and closes with the FAITH of Joseph (vv. 22-26). Joseph dies claiming God's promise that there would one day be deliverance from Egypt. "Don't leave my bones in Egypt!" he demanded. The Old Testament book of beginnings closes. But, we have another book! The New Testament begins with Matthew. That testament will close with the Revelation, man in a city, not in a coffin. And it is Jesus who makes the difference!

PRAYER: "Thank You, precious Savior, that though sin brings a coffin, Your salvation brings eternal life."

February

PROMISES MADE. PROMISES KEPT.

*Matthew is the perfect bridge between
the Old and New Testaments. The first
Gospel shows us that the Lord Jesus
fulfilled all the Old Testament predicted
about Him. Look for "fulfilled" as you
walk through Matthew in your devotions.*

FEBRUARY 1

READING: Matthew 1

" ... Jesus: for He shall save His people from their sins." Matthew 1:21

The New Testament begins with a long list of names. What kind of devotional is that? First century Jews would be very interested in it. The promised Messiah must be in the family trees of Abraham and David. This is the proof. Matthew moves from the BLOODLINE of Jesus (vv.1-17) to the BIRTH of Jesus (vv.18-25). Joseph faces a DILEMMA (vv.18-19). He was engaged to Mary but found she was expecting a baby. His fears are relieved when he has a DREAM (vv. 20-23) in which the angel of the Lord appears and assures him Mary's baby is supernaturally conceived of the Holy Spirit. And in that dream he is told the baby will be named JESUS, meaning Jehovah is salvation. So Joseph makes the right DECISION (vv. 24-25). And so Jesus is born.

PRAYER: "Thank You, heavenly Father, for sending Jesus, our Saviour."

FEBRUARY 2

READING: Matthew 2

" ... that it might be fulfilled which was spoken by the prophets, He shall be called a Nazarene." Matthew 2:23

Bethlehem. Jerusalem. Egypt. Nazareth. Wise men. Herod. Joseph. What a chapter of places and faces! Matthew 2 traces the childhood of Jesus from Bethlehem to Nazareth. Count the times the word "fulfilled" occurs. In every location and scene God is fulfilling everything He promised about the coming of the Savior. The hometown of our Lord was a little town in the hill country. Think about the PLACE of Nazareth. Nothing to brag about. Looked down upon by the Jerusalem highbrows, Nazareth is the subject of a PROMISE. The plural "prophets" seems to indicate a composite of what several said. Jesus grew up exactly where they said He would! But, of course the PERSON of Nazareth is our focus. One day He walked away and "Jesus of Nazareth" went forth to be the Savior!

PRAYER: "Lord Jesus, thank You for being the Nazarene! "

FEBRUARY 3

READING: Matthew 3

" ... this is my beloved Son, in whom I am well pleased." Matthew 3:17

There is something thrilling and moving about a young person launching his/her life's work. Jesus is ready to commence His ministry. Matthew passes over thirty years of preparation and moves to the beginning of Jesus' ministry. BAPTISM. He takes us to the ministry of John the Baptist, baptizing in the Jordan. Then, Jesus steps forth to be baptized. John demurs. But Jesus insists. What a beautiful scene. Jesus is lowered into the water then raised out of the water. What a picture of His death, burial and resurrection! BLESSEDNESS. God the Son comes out of the water; God the Holy Spirit descends upon Him like a dove; God the Father speaks approval from heaven. The Father is pleased with Him. What do you think of Him? Do you love Him enough to follow Him in baptism?

PRAYER: "Lord Jesus, You went through Calvary's baptism for me. Help me to be willing to follow You in baptism."

FEBRUARY 4

READING: Matthew 4

"Then the devil leaveth Him, and, behold, angels came and ministered unto Him." Matthew 4:11

Our greatest triumphs are often followed by our greatest temptations. Matthew 4 begins, "Then." When? After His baptism. After the baptism, the battle; after the ecstasy, the agony; after the dove, the devil! The temptation of the devil is three-fold. The appeal to the PHYSICAL (vv. 3-4), the EMOTIONAL (vv. 5-7) and the SPIRITUAL (vv. 8-10). The devil has only three moves on the chessboard of life, (See Genesis 3:6 and 1 John 2:16). And, why should he change? He is so successful! But, he meets more than his match in Jesus! Our Lord meets each one with the Word of God and the power of the Spirit. Then the angels came. Likewise, we can conquer temptation by the promises of the Word and the power of the Spirit.

PRAYER: "Thank You, mighty Savior, for showing us how to conquer the devil's attacks."

FEBRUARY 5

READING Matthew 5

> *"And He opened His mouth, and taught them, saying ..." Matthew 5:2*

Here is the greatest sermon ever preached by the greatest preacher who ever lived. The great theme is the character and conduct of those who are in the Kingdom. The key to the sermon is found in Matthew 5:20. The only kind of righteousness that gets you into the kingdom and empowers you to live like a king is the righteousness God imparts. Then, Christ can live His life in and through us. The beatitudes begin the sermon. They teach important lessons about how to live as a kingdom citizen. We are told how to ENTER the Kingdom (vv. 3-5, "poor in spirit ... mourn ... meek ..."). Then Jesus tells us how to EXPRESS the Kingdom (vv. 6-8, "hunger and thirst ... merciful ... pure in heart ..."). And, He shows us how to ENJOY the Kingdom (vv. 9-12, "peacemakers ... persecuted ... rejoice ...").

PRAYER: "Lord, You have made me a Prince, who was a Pauper."

FEBRUARY 6

READING: Matthew 6

> *" ... your Heavenly Father knoweth that ye have need of all these things." Matthew 6:32*

Jesus sets forth how the godly life is to be lived. He begins chapter 6 talking about GIVING, PRAYING, and FASTING (vv. 1-18). He constantly talks about "your Father" (12 times). He closes by telling us, "take no thought," meaning, don't worry. Worried about something today? Don't. Jesus tells us not to worry about the very things we do worry about—Food; clothing; etc. He gives us two ways to defeat worry: one, give the Lord your FIRST: "seek ye first ..." You take care of the Lord's affairs; He will take care of yours. Two, give the Lord your FUTURE: "take no thought for the morrow." He wants us to live in day-tight compartments. Did Jesus help you yesterday? He will help you today. And, He will help you tomorrow! What's your worry?

PRAYER: "Heavenly Father, I'm glad You are in control and I don't have to worry."

FEBRUARY 7

READING: Matthew 7

" ... do ye even so to them ..." Matthew 7:12

Living the Christian life involves our relationship with the Lord and with others. Jesus now turns our attention to how we treat other people. Verse 12 is called the Golden Rule. We are to put ourselves in another's place. Then, act accordingly. He takes up the matter of CRITICIZING (vv. 1-5). We shouldn't criticize others because we don't know all the facts. And, our judgment is fallible at best. Also, a critical spirit can quench the Spirit in our life. Above all, Jesus tells us not to do it. Next, he talks about WITNESSING (v. 6). We need discernment as to the timing of our witness to others. "holy ... dogs; pearls ... swine." We must not constantly witness to those who treat Christ with contempt. Then, He talks about PRAYING (vv. 7-11). How to distinguish between criticism and discernment? It takes a lot of prayer.

PRAYER: *"Lord, help me not to criticize, but to evangelize!"*

FEBRUARY 8

READING: Matthew 8

"What manner of man is this ...?" Matthew 8:27

There is a progression in Matthew's Gospel. He gives us the PERSON of the King (1-4), the PRINCIPLES of the King (5-7), now the POWER of the King (8-9). Ten miracles in two chapters show His power in the PHYSICAL realm (He can heal DISEASE) and His power in the NATURAL realm (He can rescue from DANGER.) The disciples got in a storm following Jesus! He hasn't promised us a smooth journey; He has promised a safe landing. In the storm they "came to Him" (v. 25). What does He do? What He always does. He calms the storm. Jesus speaks and the waves lie down like whipped puppies at His feet. "With Christ in the vessel, I smile at the storm." When it's all over we can say, "What manner of man is this ... ?"

PRAYER: *"Lord Jesus, it is good to know You are my storm Tamer!"*

FEBRUARY 9

READING: Matthew 9

> *"But that ye may know that the Son of man hath power on earth to forgive sins ..." Matthew 9:6*

The power of Jesus is limitless. There is nothing He can't do. There is no place He cannot work. The POWER of Jesus. Matthew shows us His power in the physical, natural and spiritual realms. The same Christ who created the sun and causes it to come up every morning can forgive your sins. The healing of the man with palsy is filled with spiritual lessons. We learn about the PARDON of Jesus (vv. 1-2). Some have called this man the paralyzed playboy. Evidently his sickness is the result of his sin. Maybe not immediately, but ultimately sickness is a result of man's fallen condition. So, what does Jesus do first? He forgives his sin! Forgiveness is an inner work, unseen by human eyes. But, He also heals the man, which can be seen. The outer work proves the inner work.

PRAYER: *"Lord Jesus, thank You for the wonderful forgiveness of sin."*

FEBRUARY 10

READING: Matthew 10

> *"And he that taketh not his cross, and followeth after me is not worthy of me." Matthew 10:38*

A disciple is a learner, a follower of Jesus. Chapter 10 might be called an instruction manual for disciples. Three groups of disciples in three ages seem to be addressed: PAST disciples (vv. 1-15), PROSPECTIVE disciples (vv. 16-23), and PRESENT disciples (vv. 24-42). Not all the instructions here are ADDRESSED to us; there are truths that are APPLIED to us. Jesus talks about our FEARS (vv. 24-31). He tells us to "fear not." He discusses our FOES (vv. 32-39). In the midst of opposition and hatred we must take up our cross and follow Jesus. But, He encourages us about our FRIENDS (vv. 40-42). Not everyone will reject our witness. You will meet many friends as you live as a disciple of Jesus.

PRAYER: *"I thank You, Lord of the cross, that I may bear a cross for You."*

FEBRUARY 11

READING: Matthew 11

"Come ... and I will give you rest." Matthew 11:28

Matthew 11 begins with the man Jesus said was the greatest ever born (v. 11). The chapter concludes with our Lord's invitation to come to Him to receive and to find rest. Need rest? Henry Thoreau said, "The mass of men lead lives of quiet desperation. "Jesus promises two kinds of rest, if we will come to Him. One is a gift; the other will cost. There is the rest of SALVATION (v. 28). Jesus gives that to us. Loaded down with sin, what a relief when He saves us and takes that burden away. Then, there is the rest of SATISFACTON (vv. 29-30). This rest we find by living for and serving Him. Living for Jesus and serving Him brings a peace, joy and love into your life you can find in no other way.

PRAYER: "Jesus, I gladly take your yoke today."

FEBRUARY 12

READING: Matthew 12

" ... in this place is One greater ..." Matthew 12:6

Conflict and controversy surrounded the Lord Jesus. The religious leaders of the nation rejected Him. Their growing hostility didn't stop until they nailed our Lord to a cross. Culture has always rejected Jesus. But, in the midst of the controversies there are three beautiful statements about the Lord Jesus. He is greater in His role as PRIEST (v. 6). No need for the Temple anymore. Jesus set aside the whole system of Sabbath keeping and the sacrifices made in the Temple. He has made the one sacrifice for sin forever (Hebrews 10:12)! He is a greater PROPHET (v. 41). Jonah preached condemnation; Jesus preached salvation! Jonah was sad people got saved; Jesus is glad when they are saved. He is greater as a POTENTATE (v. 42). Solomon was known far and wide for his great riches and his wisdom. Jesus has greater wealth and wisdom than Solomon (Colossians 2:3)!

PRAYER: "Lord, in every way I thank You that I have found You to be greater."

FEBRUARY 13

READING: Matthew 13

> *"But blessed are your eyes, for they see: and your ears, for they hear."*
> *Matthew 13:16*

Matthew 13 is a rather lengthy chapter. You may want to break it up into several readings today. But, the chapter is filled with rich truth. PARABLES. Jesus speaks seven parables. A parable has been explained as an earthly story with a heavenly meaning. That is, a picture in the physical world is used to explain a truth in the spiritual world. In these seven parables the Lord explains God's plan and purposes for this age. Jesus gives us a look at the forces at work behind the scenes. PICTURES. Enjoy the pictures Jesus paints: the sower in the field; the wheat and the tares; the mustard seed and the birds; the sneaky housewife; the hidden treasure; the pricey pearl; the dragnet. Look carefully. Prophets desired to see what you see (v.17)!

PRAYER: *"Open my eyes, O Lord, to behold the truth in these beautiful pictures."*

FEBRUARY 14

READING: Matthew 14

> *" ... This is John the Baptist; he is risen from the dead ..." Matthew 14:2*

King Herod murdered John the Baptist in cold blood. A black episode in the Bible. There are three primary actors in this tragic scene: Herod; his wife, Herodias; and John. They are the New Testament equivalent of the Old Testament Ahab, Jezebel and Elijah. A wicked king; a she-devil wife; and a courageous prophet. Herod's statement in verse 2 gives us a classic picture of the death of a conscience. Conscience. We all have one. It is the red warning light in the soul; the moral beeper that goes off when we do wrong; the alarm on our cell phone. Note the successive stages of Herod's conscience—it is a TROUBLED conscience (vv. 3-5), then a TRAPPED conscience (vv. 6-12), and finally a TORMENTED conscience (vv. 1-2). Don't tamper with your conscience.

PRAYER: *"Help me, Lord, to allow You to keep my conscience working properly by allowing Your Word to inform it."*

FEBRUARY 15

READING: Matthew 15

" ... *yet the dogs eat of the crumbs ...*" Matthew 15:27

Jesus' dealings with the woman of Canaan are indeed strange. But, the account is very helpful. Look at this AGONIZING MOTHER (vv. 21-22). Her daughter is vexed with a demon. Are you a troubled parent? Now look at an AMAZING MASTER (vv. 23-24). His response to this mother's need is unexpected. Silence. Then, He calls her a dog! Jesus is not really being harsh and cruel. He is guiding and developing her faith. So, she is just willing to take the crumbs! She sees a crack in the door and rushes through it. (v. 27). Then comes an APPEALING MIRACLE (vv. 25-28). The daughter is healed and Jesus praises the mom for great faith (v. 28). He has a love that won't let us go; we need a faith that won't let Him go!

PRAYER: *"Lord, I'd rather have the crumbs from Your table than the luxuries from the devil's table."*

FEBRUARY 16

READING: Matthew 16 " ... *Whom say ye that I am?*" Matthew 16:15

Who is Jesus? This is the perennial question (vs. 13-14) ... Everyone has an opinion about Jesus. The Lord asks His disciples what others were saying about Him—John the Baptist; Elijah; Jeremiah; or another prophet. Maybe He reminded people of John because of His PREACHING; Elijah because of His PRAYERS; Jeremiah because of His PASSION. More importantly, this is the PERSONAL question (vv. 15-16). What others say is no substitute for your personal decision. Peter declares, "You are the Christ, the Son of the living God." As Christ, Peter with divine inspiration places Him on the throne of Israel. As Son he puts Him on the throne of the universe. In response the Lord says to Peter, "Blessed ..." (v. 17). To answer the question, "Who is Jesus" correctly is to be blessed now and forever.

PRAYER: *"Blessed Lord Jesus, I willing confess You as King of the universe and King of my life."*

FEBRUARY 17

READING: Matthew 17

"... hear ye Him." Matthew 17:5

We focus on the transfiguration experience of our Lord. The experience begins with the heavenly VISION (vv. 1-2). Peter, James and John go to a high mountain with Jesus. There are degrees of nearness to Jesus. He loves all of us equally, but our response to His love is key. We can be as close to Jesus as we want to be. On the mountain, while praying (Luke 9:29), He is transfigured before them. A change on the outside that comes from the inside. All the inner glory of Jesus shone forth. Jesus can do this for our life (See 2 Corinthians 3:18). The heavenly VISITORS (vv. 3-4) appear. Moses (the law) and Elijah (the prophets) appear. The vision concludes with the heavenly VOICE (vv. 5-8). The Father is pleased with His Son. "Hear Him." If we will, many problems are solved.

PRAYER: *"Lord Jesus, speak today and I will hear and obey."*

FEBRUARY 18

READING: Matthew 18

"... despise not one of these little ones ..." Matthew 18:10

In the middle of the disciples' fuss about who is the greatest Jesus evidently calls a little child to Himself. Jesus loves children. They were attracted to Him. He talks about humility and the value of a child in God's sight. His word of caution we greatly need. "Don't despise these little ones." Children are special to God. They are SERVED by angels (v. 10). This may mean we have angels to watch over us. Whether this is so or not, it is obvious that children are the object of the angels' attention and care. Children are SOUGHT by the Lord Jesus (vv. 11-13). As the shepherd loves sheep, so the Savior loves and seeks out the little children. And, children are SEALED by the Father (v. 14). The heavenly Father wants children to be saved and belong to Him forever!

PRAYER: *"Help me, O Father, to love children as You and the Lord Jesus do."*

FEBRUARY 19

READING: Matthew 19

> *" ... he went away sorrowful: for he had great possessions."*
> *Matthew 19:22*

The rich young ruler and Jesus. The DISCUSSION. One had a lot in this world, nothing in eternity; the Other had little in this world, everything in eternity. He comes to the right Person; he asks the right question; he gets the right answer. But, he does the wrong thing. "What good thing shall I do ... eternal life?" (v. 16). The question is flawed. Salvation is based upon what Jesus did, not anything we do. Jesus responds with a question of His own, "Why callest thou me good ... ?" (v. 17). Jesus never asked questions to get information, but to teach lessons. You can't call Jesus good unless you call Him God. Jesus puts up the commandments as a mirror. The DECISION. Then, Jesus calls Him to forsake his possessions and follow Him. The young man Is "sorrowful" and walks away. What does Jesus tell us to leave to follow Him?

PRAYER: "Lord, may I let nothing between my soul and the Savior."

FEBRUARY 20

READING: Matthew 20

> *"And Jesus stood still ..." Matthew 20:32*

Jesus is going up to Jerusalem (v. 17). This was true geographically. It was also true spiritually. Crowds were taking sacrificial lambs for the Passover feast. Jesus, the Perfect Lamb, is headed to the cross! He moves forward definitely, decisively, and with great determination. Along the way He goes through Jericho. On the way out He passes 2 blind men. We know one was Bartimaeus. Jesus hears the CRY of the MEN (vv. 29-30). They cry out for mercy. That's what we need today. Jesus also hears the CRITICISM of the MULTITUDE (v. 31). How often do others keep people from Jesus. But, they don't stop the COMPASSION of the MASTER (vv. 32-34)! So, what does Jesus do? He stands still! The cry for mercy stops Deity in His tracks! With compassion, Jesus touches their eyes. And the first person they see is Jesus!

PRAYER: "Lord, I am thankful our cry for mercy is heard by You."

FEBRUARY 21

READING: Matthew 21

> *"... Hosanna to the Son of David ... Hosanna in the highest."*
> *Matthew 21:9*

The last week of Jesus' stay on earth has come. He comes to Jerusalem to die on a cross. Perhaps millions are coming into the city during Passover time. This morning Jesus dresses Himself in the mirror of prophecy. He read about the Triumphal Entry in Zechariah 9:9 and said, "That's me." So, He will ride a donkey into the city. He comes riding in LOWLINESS. Kings normally rode horses, picturing war. The Lord rides a donkey, picturing peace. He comes riding in His LOFTINESS. There is the cry of welcome and acclaim. "Hosanna" means save now. What is Jesus doing? Is His face covered with pride? No. His face is drenched with tears (See Luke 19:41). The parade of the Lord is underway today. Let us join it!

PRAYER: *"The hymn says, 'Come then and join this angel band and on to glory go.'*
Help me to join it!"

FEBRUARY 22

READING: Matthew 22

> *"... And he was speechless." Matthew 22:12*

The GRACE. Salvation is like accepting an invitation to a wedding. Jesus used weddings as parables of the offer of salvation. Israel was invited to the great feast of salvation (vv. 1-7). Everything was ready. But, those who were invited refused to come. So, there was extended a general invitation. "As many as ye shall find, bid to the marriage." (v. 9). This is God's program of world evangelism. Ours is a "whosoever will" Gospel. The GARMENT. But, salvation is a personal matter. One of those invited had no wedding garment (v. 11). The question was raised, *Why* don't you have a wedding garment? One was provided for each guest at the door. Too many try to come to Christ on their terms, not receiving the garment of salvation provided by the Lord. "Speechless." Refusal to accept God's provision leaves us without excuse.

PRAYER: *"Lord, I gladly take the garment You have provided by the blood of Calvary's*
cross."

FEBRUARY 23

READING: Matthew 23

"Woe unto you, scribes, Pharisee, hypocrites! ...." Matthew 23:13

Jesus had the tenderest heart ever to beat in a human breast. But, He was no weakling. Matthew 23 is filled with strong language, "woe ... blind guides ... fools ... offspring of vipers ... hypocrites." Jesus is unmasking the hypocrites. The word means, to play a part. Jesus unmasks hypocrisy by giving an EXPLANATION (vv. 1-12). Jesus shows hypocrisy for what it is—no SINCERITY (vv. 1-3), no EMPATHY (vv. 4), and no HUMILITY (vv. 5-12). As the stunned Pharisees, the crowd and His own disciples listen, Jesus declares a CONDEMNATION (vv. 13-33). He gives a series of eight "woes." You can hear the rolling thunder of Christ's wrath. But, was it a series of angry, bitter condemnations? No. Jesus is speaking with a broken heart. He closes with a LAMENTATION (vv. 34-39). He mourns the spiritual desolation in the Jerusalem headed for destruction.

PRAYER: *"Lord, may I never be a religious play actor."*

FEBRUARY 24

READING: Matthew 24

" ... they shall see the Son of Man coming ..." Matthew 24:30

Jesus begins and ends His earthly ministry with sermons on mountains. Today, we consider His return. Remember that the Lord's sermon about His return is not in chronological order. The INTENTION of the sermon. He presents His coming again as it relates to the 3-fold division of humanity (See I Corinthians 10:32). First, His return as it relates to the Gentile nations (vv. 1-14). Next, He presents His return as it relates to the Jews (vv. 15-35). Last, He relates His coming as it relates to the Church (vv. 36-51). The CAUTION of the sermon. We are told specifically that no one knows the day and hour (v. 36). Yet there seem to be no end of those who try to know something Jesus said they can't know! Rather than speculating about days, let us be faithful to watch and wait and work until He comes!

PRAYER: *"Lord, today, I keep my eyes on the skies as I live looking."*

FEBRUARY 25

READING: **Matthew 25**

> *"Watch therefore: for ye know not what hour your Lord doth come."*
> *Matthew 25:42*

J esus was the Master Teacher. Truth came alive as He used vivid illustrations, many in parables (an earthly story with a heavenly meaning). The truths of Matthew 24 are illustrated by the parables of Matthew 25. The PEOPLE. The first one is the parable about the 10 virgins awaiting the coming of the Bridegroom and the wedding celebration. Five were wise; five were foolish. The difference? Five had oil in their lamps; five didn't. When the Bridegroom tarried, they went to sleep. We are living in the days of delay. Not from God's perspective, but from ours. And there are some spiritually sleepy people! Ah, but the midnight cry, "Behold, the Bridegroom cometh." The PREPARATION. Now, the question: do you have the oil? The oil points to the indwelling presence of the Holy Spirit. Are you ready?

PRAYER: *"Lord, thank You I can be saved and ready for the Lord's return. Maybe today!"*

FEBRUARY 26

READING: **Matthew 26**

> *"... nevertheless not as I will, but as you will." Matthew 26:39*

T he moon is full. Jesus takes His disciples through narrow Jerusalem streets, out the gate, down the hill through the brook Kidron, into a garden known as Gethsemane, meaning oil press. There the Savior will be crushed like an olive that the oil of salvation might flow. Gethsemane was an enclosed garden (See John 18:1). Indeed, much that transpires here is closed to us. Think of Gethsemane's TRAUMA (vv. 36-38). "Sorrowful ... very heavy ... exceeding sorrowful ..." Traumatic words indeed! But, words of TRIUMPH: Thy will be done! Judas brings Gethsemane's TREACHERY (vv. 47-54). A kiss, intended to convey affection, conveys betrayal. We see also Gethsemane's TRAGEDY (vv. 55-56). The disciples all flee. He is left alone. Betrayed and abandoned. Have you had a Gethsemane? Sooner or later we all go to the Garden of Gethsemane.

PRAYER: *"Lord, may I be willing to renounce my will and surrender to Yours."*

FEBRUARY 27

READING: Matthew 27

" ... and led Him away to crucify Him." Matthew 27:31

Jesus was crucified at Golgotha, the Hebrew word (Latin is Calvary), meaning place of a skull. There Jesus died by crucifixion, no ordinary death (See Philippians 2:8). Though the hill may not have been high geographically, theologically and spiritually it is the highest hill in human history. Think about Golgotha's CROWDS (vv. 32-44). Simon, a passerby, was there by compulsion. Calloused soldiers were there, gambling for His garments, little realizing they were fulfilling Scripture (See Psalm 22:18). Two thieves were there (vv. 37-44). Both condemned, one converted (See Luke 23:42-43). And there are Golgotha's CRIES (vv. 45-53). They are cries of mystery and victory. Then, Golgotha's CROWNS (vv. 54-61). The Centurion affirms Him, "Truly this was the Son of God" (v. 54). Joseph gently takes His body down from the cross. Joseph is silent no more (John 9:38)!

PRAYER: *"Help me today to boldly declare the good news about Jesus."*

FEBRUARY 28

READING: Matthew 28

"He is not here: for He is risen." Matthew 28:6

Jesus was buried in a borrowed tomb (See Matthew 27:60). The Rock of Ages in an aging rock! The Light of the world now shrouded in darkness. This tomb was intended to be a SECURE tomb (See Matthew 27:62-66). This secured tomb was intended by men to prevent a hoax. God's purpose is to prove the reality of the resurrection. The tomb becomes a SHAKEN tomb (28:1-4). God sent down His earthquake angel to roll back the stone. The stone was rolled away, not to let Jesus out, but to let the disciples in! No power on earth can hold Jesus in that rock casket. For millions that tomb is now a SPECIAL tomb (28:5-15). The angel speaks in the past tense. He was there, but He isn't anymore! The truth of the matter is, the tomb is empty!

PRAYER: *"Thank You, Lord, that the tomb is empty."*

FEBRUARY 29

READING: Matthew 28

"Go ye therefore ..." Matthew 28:19

The Risen Lord is going back to heaven. These are the closing words of our Lord and of Matthew's Gospel. These words of our Lord, called the Great Commission, are the church's marching orders until He returns. The Lord Jesus sets forth His POWER (v. 18). "All power" means all authority. He declares His universal authority ("in heaven and in earth"). Jesus is in charge! What an encouragement to us today. The task of getting His Gospel to the whole world is daunting. But, His heavenly resources are at our disposal. His PLAN (vv. 19-20a) is simple. Going. Winning. Baptizing. Teaching. The church must be going to win the lost, baptizing them and then teaching them to observe the Lord's commands. We are assured of His PRESENCE (vv. 20b). "Lo, I am with you." If you will accept His "Go", you can have His "Lo!"

PRAYER: *"Today, Lord, I want to be on the go for You."*

March

JOURNEY.

Exodus means, the way out. As God led Israel out of the land of Egypt, so He leads us out of the land of sin. Genesis tells us how humankind got into sin. Exodus tells us how to get out!

MARCH 1

READING: Exodus 1

> *"Now there arose up a new king over Egypt, which knew not Joseph."*
> *Exodus 1:8*

Exodus begins with "now" tying to Genesis. Israel is "now" in Egypt. This opening chapter presents the DESIGNATION of a people (vv. 1-7). The names may not be of interest to you. They were certainly of interest to those mentioned! They were in Egypt because of Joseph But, Joseph died! Trouble for Israel. We also learn about the DOMINATION of a people (vv. 8-10). There's a new king in town with no appreciation for Joseph, nor his people. We are living in a world which knows not Jesus and has no appreciation for Him nor His people. We also are taught concerning the DESPERATION of a people (vv. 15-22). Forced into slave labor, Israel's affliction gets worse and worse. Now comes the final dastardly plan—all the boy babies must go into the crocodile-infested Nile (v. 22).

PRAYER: *"Lord, help me understand where I live."*

MARCH 2

READING: Exodus 2

> *" ... when she saw that he was a goodly child, she hid him 3 months."*
> *Exodus 2:2*

All the boy babies are to be cast into the Nile River. Deliverance needed. How does God deliver them? He sends a baby! Our deliverance? He sent a baby, His only begotten Son. Moses, one of the most important people in the Bible, steps onstage. Think about Moses' PRESERVATION (vv. 1-6). He is sheltered in a godly home. Every child needs one. But, the Nile is unavoidable. What does his mother do? She places him in an ark. Our children face the world. We must get them into the Ark of Salvation. Consider Moses' EDUCATION (vv. 7-10). Moses received his spiritual education from his godly mother, his secular education in Pharaoh's house (See Acts 7:22). Then Moses' ISOLATION (vv. 15b-25). Moses has a 40-year leadership course in the wilderness.

PRAYER: *"Lord, You are preparing me for what You are preparing for me."*

MARCH 3

READING: Exodus 3

> *"... the bush burned with fire, and the bush was not consumed."*
> *Exodus 3:2*

Moses' life consists of three equal 40-year parts: Prince of Egypt; Shepherd in Midian; Leader of God's people. Someone said Moses went from somebody to nobody to somebody! Never a day like this before. He has no idea he will meet God this day. But, a desert place becomes a Divine place. Moses has a Divine APPOINTMENT (vv. 1-5). A common bush begins to shine with a blaze of the Divine. An ordinary bush, yet ablaze with the fire of God. Out of the flaming bush God calls Moses with the double knock, "Moses, Moses." (v. 4). Shoeless Moses stands on holy ground. God's presence calls for reverence. Moses hears a Divine ANNOUNCEMENT (vv. 6-8). God announces He is ready to deliver His people. Moses receives a Divine ASSIGNMENT (vv. 9-10). "I will send thee ..." God has an assignment for you.

PRAYER: *"Lord, make this ordinary day an extraordinary day."*

MARCH 4

READING: Exodus 6

> *"I will harden Pharaoh's heart, and multiply my signs and my*
> *wonders ..." Exodus 6:3*

Moses and Pharaoh are in mortal combat. Moses commands Pharaoh to let the people go. Pharaoh is not about to do it. The PLAGUES. The ten plagues recorded in Exodus show that God is pressing the battle to the center of Egypt's idolatry. The Lord God is the true God. The gods of Egypt are false. Blood! Frogs! Gnats! Flies! Dead cattle! Boils! Hail! Locusts! Darkness! Death! All these plagues challenge a false deity. The PHARAOH. There is another purpose of the plagues—to show what is in Pharaoh's heart. His heart is "hardened." The word means, twisting, as one would a rope. God is twisting Pharaoh's heart, squeezing out what is in it. Sometimes Pharaoh hardens his own heart; other times God does it. God is giving Pharaoh what he chooses. God has given you a choice.

PRAYER: *"Lord, help me to choose what You lovingly desire for me."*

MARCH 5

READING: Exodus 12

" ... a lamb ... the lamb ... your lamb ..." Exodus 12: 3-5

God will lead His people out of Egypt. The lamb is in view. There is a beautiful progression here: a lamb ... the lamb ... your lamb." Jesus is not a Savior; He is The Savior; is He your Savior? Jesus is presented in the New Testament as The Lamb (See John 1:29). This Passover lamb is a PERSONAL lamb (vv. 3-5). Each individual had to be in the house where the lamb was. The Passover lamb is a SACRIFICIAL lamb (vv. 5-13). The lamb had to be slain. God said, "When I see the blood ..." (v. 13). Our Lamb shed His blood for us (See Hebrews 9:22). The Passover lamb is a MEMORIAL lamb (v. 14). Passover looked back to what God had done for them. We gather at the Lord's Table to remember what Jesus did for us (See 1 Corinthians 11:26).

PRAYER: *"O lamb of God, thank You for Your shed blood."*

MARCH 6

READING: Exodus 14

" ... and the waters were divided" Exodus 14:21

The children of Israel are headed to the Promised Land. But, just ahead is the Red Sea. God's greatness and power is seen in what God did there. There is a PROBLEM (vv. 1-9). God often leads us, not by the nearest way, but by the way best for us. The problem gets bigger. Pharaoh is coming. They are between the devil and the deep Red Sea! The people PANIC (vv. 10-18). They cry to the Lord (v. 10) and criticize Moses (vv. 11-12). This happens when we see God through our problems instead of seeing our problems through God. God's POWER is displayed (vv. 19-31). God miraculously parts the waters. Taking miracles out of the Bible is like taking heat out of fire, notes out of music or numbers out of math. When God parts the waters, don't forget to PRAISE (Exodus 15).

PRAYER: *"Help me see the 'footprints of Jesus, that make the pathway glow'."*

MARCH 7

READING: Exodus 16

" ... ye shall be filled with bread ..." Exodus 16:12

God is matriculating His people in Wilderness University. A 40-year curriculum! We develop character in difficult circumstances. They learn the Lord is with them in the wilderness. Living for Jesus in our weary world we find God will meet our every need. God provides them with MANNA (The WORD of GOD, see verse 12). We can feed our souls daily with fresh bread from heaven's ovens. But, note it had to be gathered daily. Yesterday's Bible reading won't do. We must feed on the Word daily. God also provides them with WATER (The SPIRIT of GOD, see 17:1-7). When Moses smote the rock the water began to flow. That Rock was Christ (See 1 Corinthians 10:4). Because of the death of Christ the Holy Spirit of God flows into our life, filling and refreshing us.

PRAYER: *"O Lord, thank You for Your provision in this weary wilderness world in which we live."*

MARCH 8

READING: Exodus 20

"And God spake all these words, saying, ..." Exodus 20:1

Sinai looms before the Israelites. There God will give the law through Moses. The second part of Exodus gives the law. The law is divided into two parts: the MORAL (Ten Commandments) and the CIVIL (Exodus 21-23) law. The Ten Commandments encode the moral law. There are NEGATIVE words— "Thou shalt not ..." The very things God says not to do, we do! Proof we are sinners needing a Savior. His law is also POSITIVE—each expresses who God is and what He is like. God's law is INCLUSIVE—they hold together (See James 2:10). Like a chain, break one and they all are broken. These Ten Commandments were written on tablets of stone. They are also written somewhere else—in every human heart (See Romans 2:15). We actually don't "break" God's law. Violate them and sooner or later they will "break" us.

PRAYER: *"Father, the law says, 'do,' Grace says, 'done'."*

MARCH 9

READING: Exodus 20

"Thou shalt have no other gods before me." Exodus 20:2-3

The Ten Commandments are remarkably concise, 297 words in all. The first one makes an assertion, issues a prohibition and gives an invitation. We learn here about the REALITY of God ("I am ..."). He wants us to know who He is; what kind of God He is. The first commandment assumes the existence of God. The Bible never attempts to prove His existence (See Psalm 14:1). We learn about the RIVALS to God ("no other gods ..."). Israel's problem wasn't atheism (no God), but polytheism (many gods). All worship God or gods. It is true that man is "incurably religious." These other gods are "before Me." To be loyal to any other god (money; possessions; pleasures) is to be disloyal to the true God. This command suggests the REVERENCE for God ("have"). God says, if you will have no other gods, you can have Me!

PRAYER: *"Help me, Lord, to serve You and You alone."*

MARCH 10

READING: Exodus 20

"Thou shalt not make unto thee any graven image, or any likeness ..." Exodus 20:4-6

The first two commandments are closely related. We learn first, who God is. Then, we learn how to worship Him. The second commandment PROHIBITS ("... not make ... not bow down ..."). God says, don't make an image of Me, nor worship a god someone else makes. Humankind has the tendency to make representations of God. This distorts and degrades God. It PROTECTS ("... the Lord thy God am a jealous God ..."). God is jealous of that special relationship He wants with us. God will have no rivals, allow no competition. It also PROJECTS ("upon the children"). Incorrect worship can bring misery upon our offspring. Proper worship will bring mercy! We meet God, not in images of wood and stone, but in the Person of Jesus Christ. We need no other image.

PRAYER: *"Help me to worship You correctly, dear Lord, not just for my sake, but for my children and grandchildren."*

MARCH 11

READING: Exodus 20

> *"Thou shalt not take the name of the Lord thy God in vain ..."*
> *Exodus 20:7*

Two of the Ten Commandments deal with sins of the tongue. This one and the ninth. God has given us the beautiful gift of speech. But, it is possible to misuse this gift to curse man (See James 3:9), or even sadder, to abuse the name of God. God's name can be desecrated in a number of ways. By PROFANITY. What a common sin. We hear it from all directions—daily speech; TV; music. Profanity shows utter disregard for God's holy name and a disregard for others. By DISHONESTY. Using God's name in oaths to cover dishonesty means adding God's name to a lie. By INSINCERITY. To talk of God with our lips, but deny Him with our life violates this commandment. But, the negative suggest the positive! Jesus teaches us to pray, "Hallowed by your name." (Matthew 6:9).

PRAYER: *"Lord, guard my lips to honor Thy name."*

MARCH 12

READING: Exodus 20

> *"Remember the sabbath day, to keep it holy."* Exodus 20:8

The first four commandments tie together, focusing upon our relationship to God. The SABBATH. God wants us to reserve a day to worship Him. The tendency is to go to two extremes: To make our day of worship a day of gloom and burden. God didn't say, "Thou shalt be miserable on the sabbath." The other tendency is to make it just like any other day. The day of worship is too often sacrificed on the altars of profit and pleasure. The Sabbath is Jewish, commemorating creation. Christians worship on the first day, commemorating resurrection. The SAVIOR. Christianity has transformed the day of worship from shadow to substance (See Colossians 2:14); from Saturday to Sunday (See Acts 20:7); from Sabbath to the Savior (See Hebrews 4). In the Old Testament it was work, then rest. Now it is rest, then work!

PRAYER: *"Thank You, Lord, I may worship You, not just one day, but every day."*

MARCH 13

READING: Exodus 20

"Honor thy father and thy mother ..." Exodus 20:12

The previous four commandments focused on our relationship with God. The next six deal with our relationships with others. First and primary is our relationship to our parents. Family is the basic structure of civilization. Relationship to parents has a primary influence in your life. How you relate to them will affect every other relationship in life. This command is not optional, but essential. To "honor" means to hold in high esteem. To honor them involves our RESPONSE. All of Scripture tells us to obey them. If you don't learn to obey your parents, you may well have problems with obeying authority in school, work and government. To honor also involves RESPECT. Some parents are unworthy of honor. But, they may be honored for their role, not their behavior. Obedience to parents tends to a long life. Rebellion against parents can cause a lot of problems along the way.

PRAYER: "Lord, I choose to honor my parents."

MARCH 14

READING: Exodus 20

"Thou shalt not kill." Exodus 20:13

Human life is sacred, so He says, "Don't kill." Little value is placed upon human life in our culture. Killing is more involved than you may think. Killing involves OUTWARDNESS. This is the kind of killing involving an act. Homicide—the killing of another human being. Abortion—the killing of the unborn. Secondary killing—in indirect ways such as drunken driving and the sale of alcohol and drugs. Killing involves INWARDNESS. There is also the attitude of killing. Jesus said killing originates in the heart (See Matthew 19:18). Sin is gloated over in the heart before it is acted out in the body. Thankfully, those who have killed can receive FORGIVENESS. We are told that the blood of Jesus cleanses from ALL sin (See 1John 1:7). All of us are guilty of the greatest killing ever done. Your sins and mine killed Jesus on the cross.

PRAYER: "Thank You, Father, for forgiving me of the killing of Your Son."

MARCH 15

READING: Exodus 20

"Thou shalt not commit adultery." Exodus 20:14

Our culture is sex-saturated. So this commandment is scorned, belittled, assaulted and ignored. And the result? Rather than being associated with beautiful words like love, marriage, and babies, sex is linked with words like rape, prostitution, perversion and disease. This negative commandment has a positive purpose. We should keep ourselves sexually pure for NATIONAL reasons. No nation can survive sexual immorality. And, for MARITAL reasons. This generation speaks more about love and understands it less than any previous one. This command draws a circle around marriage and teaches the sacredness of sex within that relationship. But, we should keep it for PERSONAL reasons as well. A host of mental, spiritual and psychological consequences go with sexual immorality. Have you broken that commandment? The words of Jesus to the adulterous woman are for us as well, "Go and sin no more." (John 8:11).

PRAYER: *"Help me, Lord Jesus, to keep myself pure in deed and in thought."*

MARCH 16

READING: Exodus 20

"Thou shalt not steal." Exodus 20:15

On the surface this commandment seems clear-cut and simple. But, deeper reflection makes it more extensive. Stealing is taking that which does not belong to you. There are several ways to steal. There is the matter of PROPERTY. The Bible does assume your right to own things. Though God has ultimate ownership, He has given things to us for our trusteeship. There is the matter of DISHONESTY. We may steal by shoplifting, refusing to pay bills, cheating in school, etc. We may steal by stealing another's reputation or name. We can even steal from God (See Malachi 3:8-10). Jesus puts this in a positive manner when He says, "whatsoever ye would that men should do to you, do ye even so to them ..." (Matthew 7:12). The greatest theft of all is to refuse to give to God our life.

PRAYER: *"Owner of my life, may I not steal it from You."*

MARCH 17

READING: Exodus 20

"Thou shalt not bear false witness ..." Exodus 20:16

This commandment could be translated, "You must not lie." Lying seems to be an accepted method of procedure in all areas of life. Let's DEFINE lying. To lie is to make a statement contrary to fact with the intention to deceive. We all tend to be liars (See Psalm 58:3). Seems to go with our fallen nature, doesn't it? Let's DESCRIBE lying. Slandering is telling an intentional, malicious lie about another person. Tale bearing is to make up an untrue tale against another person, spread by rumor-mongering and gossip. Gossips are the verbal pests of society—buzzing, swarming, stinging. Flattering is another form of lying. Flattery is like perfume. It's ok to smell it, but don't swallow it! But, we can DEFEAT lying by positively telling the truth. The Bible commands us to speak the truth in love (See Ephesians 4:15). Let's commit today to being a truthful person.

PRAYER: "Lord, help me be a truth teller."

MARCH 18

READING: Exodus 20

"Thou shalt not covet ..." Exodus 20:17

This tenth and last commandment differs from the other nine in that it is primarily inward, rather than outward. Nine deal with sins of action; this one with sins of attitude. Nine are visible; this one is invisible. To covet means the desire to have more. Covetousness is the mother of all others. To covet is a HEART sin. Jesus said it comes from within (See Mark 7:21-22). This poisonous plant has roots deep in the soil of our sinful hearts. To covet is a HIDDEN sin. 1 Thessalonians 2:5 talks about a "cloak of covetousness." To covet is a HIDEOUS sin. Romans 1:29 places it between wickedness and maliciousness. The good news is that covetousness may be replaced. The opposite of covetousness is contentment. God can cause us to be content with what He has provided for us (See Hebrews 13:5-6).

PRAYER: "Lord, I will be content with what You provide today."

MARCH 19

READING: Exodus 32

"Go, get thee down; for thy people ... have corrupted themselves."
Exodus 32:7

Before Moses returned, Israel had broken most of the commandments. We see the people CORRUPTED (vv. 1-14). The people grew restless during the long six weeks of Moses' absence. They demand a golden calf to worship and Aaron obliges. An idol they can own, handle and control. The tendency is to make a god of something we can see. The bonds of restraint are broken and anything goes. Sounds like society today, doesn't it? But, the people are CONFRONTED (vv. 15-28). When Moses was coming down the mountain he heard the noise. The people are whirling around the shameful idol. Smashed tablets. Bitter powder. Sin cannot be taken lightly. Verse 20 teaches that sooner or later we will have to taste the consequences of sin. God doesn't add Sweet and Low to overcome the bitter taste of sin.

PRAYER: *"Lord, may I not make an idol of anything today."*

MARCH 20

READING: Exodus 33

" ... show me thy glory" Exodus 33:18

This is the most glorious moment n Moses' life. God reveals two wonderful truths to him in this chapter: grace (vv. 12-17) and glory (vv. 18-23). God gives Moses a glimpse of His glory. He had seen the glory cloud. He desires a deeper vision of God's glory. God's glory is the outward manifestation of His inward reality. God is invisible. When He chooses to reveal Himself the word to describe it is glory. We see God's glory in the INCARNATION of Christ (See John 1:14), the CRUCIFIXION of Christ (See Luke 24:26), the RESURRECTION of Christ (See 1 Peter 1:21), and in the EXALTATION of Christ (See 1 Timothy 3:16). Have you seen the glory? "Turn your eyes upon Jesus, look full in His wonderful face; and the things of earth will grow strangely dim, in the light of His glory and grace."

PRAYER: *"Lord, may I glimpse Your glory today."*

MARCH 21

READING: Exodus 34

" ... the skin of his face shone ..." Exodus 34:30

After Moses got a glimpse of God's glory his face was shining. We are told of three shining faces in the Bible: Moses' face REFLECTED God's glory (See 2 Corinthians 3); Stephen's face RADIATED God's glory (See Acts 6:15); Jesus' face REVEALED God's glory (See Matthew 17:2). God's children can reflect the glory of God in their lives. 2 Corinthians 3:18 tells us how. The child of God looks into the Word of God (a glass), sees the Son of God and is changed by the Spirit of God. Moses didn't realize his face was reflecting God's glory. As believers grow in the Lord others will see Jesus in their life. They aren't aware of it, but all those around them are aware of God's presence shining forth in their life. Today are we reflections of the Christ who lives within us?

PRAYER: *"Lord, may my life daily be a reflection of Your glory."*

MARCH 22

READING: Exodus 25

"And let them make me a sanctuary; that I may dwell among them" Exodus 25:8

We must step back a few chapters to pick up the account of the construction of the Tabernacle in the wilderness. This structure was to be designed according to God's specific pattern. There God said He would dwell among His people, Israel. This was a LITERAL building (vv. 1-7). The building actually existed. Elaborate details, designs and dimensions are given for it. It was also a SPIRITUAL building (v. 8). "Sanctuary" means a sacred place, a place set apart. When finished, God's glory filled the place. And God would dwell there among His people. But, it was also a TYPICAL building (v. 9). "According to the pattern," said God. The Tabernacle pictures Christ, who came to dwell among us (See John 1:14); and the Christian (See 1 Corinthians 6:19). God now indwells us!

PRAYER: *"Lord, make my life a holy sanctuary where You feel at home today."*

MARCH 23

READING: Exodus 27:1-8; 38:1-7

"And he made the altar of burnt offering ..." Exodus 38:1

Entering the Tabernacle environs the first piece of furniture we see is the brazen altar. This altar was the largest piece in the entire Tabernacle. There the animal sacrifices were consumed by fire. The altar tells the story of a CONVICTED SINNER. Imagine an Israelite approaching that altar aware of his own sinfulness. It is all brass, reminding of judgment. But, there is a CONSECRATED SUBSTITUTE. He brings an animal with him. He lays his hands upon the animal and then it is slain in his place. Thus, there is a COMPLETED SACRIFICE. As the animal is consumed the sinner realizes that by this sacrifice a holy God is satisfied and a sinful man is justified. How wonderful to know we have a substitute—the Lord Jesus Christ.

PRAYER: *"Dear Savior, I am thankful I can come to You, not because of what I have done, but because of what You have done."*

MARCH 24

READING: Exodus 30:17-21

"Thou shalt also make a laver ..." Exodus 30:18

Just beyond the altar stands the brazen laver. The WASHING. The worshiper faces the laver as one for whom the sacrifice has been made at the brazen altar. The laver is a place for washing. The altar represents the place of substitution. The laver represents the place of sanctification. Attention shifts from the sinner to the priests. They only could wash at the laver. The WORD. Our salvation has brought about a change. We are now priests (See 1 Peter 2:9; Revelation 1:6)! We now may come daily to the laver of the Word of God for cleansing (See Ephesians 5:26). We live in a dirty world (See James 1:27). We need daily washing in the Word (See John 15:3).

PRAYER: *"Lord, I come to the Word today that I might be clean for You."*

MARCH 25

READING: Exodus 37:10-16; Leviticus 24:5-9

"And he made the table ..." Exodus 37:10

Today we enter into the first room of the tabernacle proper—the Holy Place. Once within we notice an immediate change. Everything is covered with gold! Gold speaks of God's Deity. The first article of furniture to catch our eye is the table. On the table we see freshly baked showbread. The priests can take the bread and eat it. This table is rich in meaning for us. The table is a picture of the satisfaction we find in the Lord Jesus. In Christ we have ENJOYMENT. In Christ we have fellowship with the Father and the family of God. We also have ENLIGHTENMENT. The bread on the table teaches us that our nourishment comes from Christ, the Bread of Life. How wonderful to know that the deepest hungers in our life can be satisfied by Christ. And it teaches we have ENRICHMENT. The bread provides nourishment. But, it must be eaten. The table is ready. "Come and dine!"

PRAYER: *"Bread of heaven, feed me 'till I want no more."*

MARCH 26

READING: Exodus 25:31-40

"And thou shalt make a candlestick ..." Exodus 25:31

In the holy place, opposite the table burned brightly a lampstand. This golden stand had seven lights kept constantly burning by the priests. This was the only light. The lampstand represents the illumination we have in Christ. He is our light. And we are to be lights. He makes us like Himself. He is light; we are light. Learn here about the lampstand's FUEL. The light is fueled by "pure olive oil," symbolic of the Holy Spirit. As the light was refueled daily, so we must daily seek the filling of the Spirit. Then there is the lampstand's FLAME. There could be no shining unless there was burning. And we cannot shine for Jesus unless we are willing to let the flame of the Spirit consume us (See John 5:35).

PRAYER: *"Holy Spirit, burn out all self, so I may shine for Jesus."*

MARCH 27

READING: Exodus 30:1-10,34-38

"And thou shalt make an altar to burn incense upon ..." Exodus 30:1

Directly in front of the veil before the Holy of Holies is the golden incense altar. The golden altar speaks of intercession. We have the marvelous privilege of prayer. The incense on the altar was burned, causing sweet-smelling smoke to fill the whole room. This is a beautiful picture of the SAVIOR'S prayers. Christ, our High Priest, is now in heaven praying for us (See Hebrews 7:25). It also speaks of the BELIEVER'S prayers. Our prayers can be fragrant before the Lord. There is fire. We must have passion in our prayers. They are offered morning and evening. There must be persistence in our prayers. The incense is burned "before the Lord." There must be praise in our prayers. The priests' garments were fragrant. There should be the sweet fragrance of prayer in our life.

PRAYER: *"Today may my life have about it the sweet fragrance of prayer."*

MARCH 28

READING: Exodus 25:10-16

"And they shall make an ark ..." Exodus 25:10

The innermost room of the tabernacle is the Holy of Holies. The first thing we see is a gold-plated ark with a golden lid (tomorrow!). It points to the PERSON of Christ (vv. 10-11). Wood covered in gold. Christ's humanity and deity. Perfectly blended. Christ is very man of very man, very God of very God. The God-man! We see the POSITION of Christ (vv. 12-15). The ark was made first. So, Christ is central in our faith. The ark was also foremost. The ark led the way in Israel's journeys. Christ present, prominent, and pre-eminent! Here is the PROVISION of Christ (vv. 16). Inside the ark were the tables of the covenant. The law of God is hidden in Christ's heart. A pot of golden manna. We feast on hidden manna. Aaron's rod that budded. A glorious resurrection future!

PRAYER: *"Lord, You are my Ark. I trust You for my food and future!"*

MARCH 29

READING: Exodus 25:17-22

"And thou shalt make a mercy seat ..." Exodus 25:17

The Mercy Seat is the golden lid covering the ark. It was a slab of solid gold. It points us to Christ who became our mercy seat at the cross (See Hebrews 9:5). The word means propitiation or place where satisfaction is made. The Mercy Seat was a place of ENTHRONEMENT. Israel was told this is God's dwelling place on the earth (See Psalm 99:1; Exodus 25:22). The ark testified to God's law. The Mercy Seat speaks of His grace. The Mercy Seat was also a place of ATONEMENT. On the Day of Atonement (See Leviticus 16:2, 15-17) the High Priest would sprinkle the blood of the sacrificial lamb upon and before the Mercy Seat. At Calvary Christ shed His blood for our sins (See Romans 3:25). God's law was satisfied and His love was magnified.

PRAYER: *"Dear Lord Jesus, thank You for being my Mercy Seat."*

MARCH 30

READING: Exodus 28

" ... that he may minister unto me in the priest's office ..." Exodus 28:1

Israel had prophets, who spoke to the people on behalf of God. They also had priests, who spoke to God on behalf of the people. Every believer is a priest (See 1 Peter 2:9; Revelation 1:6). Priests are CALLED. No one just decided to be a priest (See Hebrews 5:1, 4). In salvation God calls us to serve Him. Priests are CLOTHED. Aaron had seven pieces of clothing in all. We are clothed with the beautiful garments of salvation (See Isaiah 61:10). Priests are CONSECRATED. Washed with water; anointed with oil; sprinkled with blood. Priests are COMMISSIONED. We can now offer up spiritual sacrifices to the Lord (See 1 Peter 2:5). We offer Him ourselves (See Romans 12:1), our gifts (See Philippians 4:18) and our praise (See Hebrews 13:15).

PRAYER: *"Father, thank You I no longer need a priest. You have made me one!"*

MARCH 31

READING: Exodus 40

> *"... and the glory of the Lord filled the tabernacle." Exodus 40:34*

G enesis closes in gloom. Exodus ends in glory. Exodus opens with bondage; it ends with blessing. When the tabernacle was constructed "according to the pattern" God filled the house with His glory. The Lord's presence was symbolized by that visible, glorious cloud. We learn here WHEN the glory comes (40:1-33). Only when we do things His way. We learn WHERE the glory comes (40:34-35). We see God's glory in Christ (See Luke 9:32), in the church (See Ephesians 3:21), and in the Christian (See Colossians 1:27). We learn WHY the glory comes (40:36-38). God's glory in our life is evidence we belong to Him and that He is in our life. We will see glory in another place. Glory awaits us in heaven (See Revelation 21:2-3, 10-11, 23)!

PRAYER: *"Lord, I thank You that You have come to dwell in me."*

April

INFANT'S PROGRESS.

The book of Acts is the exciting account of the beginning of the church age. The baby church begins to grow and expand. Follow this thrilling story as the church moves out to fulfill the Great Commission.

APRIL 1

READING: Acts 1:1-12

" ... ye shall be witnesses unto me ..." Acts 1:8

A cts could well be called the power book. Dr. Luke, beloved physician and author of the third Gospel re-iterates the Lord's promise of the power of the Holy Spirit (See Luke 24:49). He gives us the PURPOSE of Acts (2:1-3). The disciples are continuing the work of the Lord Jesus as He works in and through them. He gives the PROMISE of Acts (2:4-8). The Holy Spirit will come upon them that they might be witnesses. A witness is someone who has seen something and can say something. We who have met Jesus can tell others about Him! But, most of all, he tells us about the PERSON of Acts (2:9-12). The focus is on Jesus as He ascended back to heaven. Keep your eyes on Jesus.

PRAYER: *"Lord Jesus, You want me to tell others about You. I will, in the power of the Holy Spirit."*

APRIL 2

READING: Acts 1:13-26

"These all continued with one accord in prayer ..." Acts 1:14

O ur Bible bus moves slowly for the first few days of the month. We want to understand the power dynamics in how the church begins the work of the Savior on the earth. From the mountain of ascension we follow the disciples to an upper room in Jerusalem. Principles emerge for God's power. The SUPPLICATION principle (vv. 13-14). The early church prayed ten days, preached ten minutes and 3,000 were saved. We preach ten days, pray ten minutes and wonder why so little happens! The SCRIPTURE principles (vv. 15-19). Peter stands with Old Testament in hand and applies it to the current situation. This book from the past has answers for our present. The SELECTION principle (vv. 20-24). Matthias was to fill Judas' place. Did they make a mistake? Think about it.

PRAYER: *"Lord, You have given me a book to guide me and a Person to lead me."*

APRIL 3

READING: Acts 2:1-41

"And when the day of Pentecost was fully come ..." Acts 2:1

Too many churches (and Christians) are bogged down between Calvary and Pentecost. They have been to Calvary for pardon, but not to Pentecost for power. Bethlehem means God WITH us; Calvary, God FOR us. Pentecost, God IN us. We learn in these verses the MEANING of Pentecost (vv. 1-13). It came fifty days after the Passover. On this day the Holy Spirit came in fulfillment of prophecy (See John 14:16-17). Peter delivered the MESSAGE of Pentecost (vv. 14-36). What a mighty message! He explains Scripture and exalts the Savior! The Lord performs the MIRACLE of Pentecost (vv. 37-41). What was the miracle? The wind? The fire? The tongues? No. All these were temporary and passed off the scene. The great miracle was the miracle of the salvation of 3,000 souls!

PRAYER: *"Holy Spirit, use me to bring to others the miracle of salvation."*

APRIL 4

READING: Acts 2:37-47

"And they continued stedfastly ..." Acts 2:42

The early church is a dream church. We see here church as it is meant to be. There is more to church than one big day. Three thousand souls saved and baptized certainly is sensational and inspiring. But, these summary verses show us the essential ingredients of a true church. First, a CONVERTED MEMBERSHIP (vv. 37-41). The members of the church were "added" (v. 41). Who added them? "The Lord added ..." (v. 47). Second, a CONSTANT MINISTRY (vv. 42-45). "apostles' doctrine ... fellowship ... breaking of bread ... prayers." Teaching, sharing, remembering, and praying! The four marks of a healthy church. Third, a CONTINUAL MULTIPLICATION (vv. 46-47). The church witnesses and the Lord adds to their number. To see people come to Christ and be added to our church is a dream come true!

PRAYER: *"Lord Jesus, thank You for giving me a church where I may witness and worship. Help me to help it become all You intend it to be."*

APRIL 5

READING: Acts 3

" ... such as I have give I thee ..." Acts 3:6

We move quickly today to the Beautiful Gate of the Temple. Peter and John are going to pray. Look at the MAN at the Gate (vv. 2-3). Lame. This is our challenge—the cripples at the gate. All around us, crippled by addiction, materialism, lust, etc. Watch the MIRACLE at the Gate (vv. 4-11). Peter gives the man what he needs, not what he wants. Peter isn't apologizing; he's bragging! Hear the MESSAGE at the Gate (vv. 12-26). That's the main event. Not the miracle, but the message. Peter turns the attention to the Lord Jesus. He faithfully preaches the good news of His crucifixion and resurrection. And, shares the thrilling truth that Jesus will come again! To heal lameness is a wonderful miracle. To heal lostness is the greater miracle (See John 14:12).

PRAYER: *"Thank You, Lord, that I have something to offer that is better than silver and gold."*

APRIL 6

READING: Acts 4

" ... the place was shaken where they were assembled together ..." Acts 4:31

The latter part of Acts 4 is quite a contrast to the former part. Peter and John are before the Sanhedrin. Now, they are in a prayer meeting. From the place of peril to the place of prayer. From scorn and threatening, to fellowship and love. What a prayer meeting! Look at the PEOPLE (v. 23). Peter and John, released, go to where other believers are gathered. Where do you go when you are "let go?" Listen to the PRAYER (vv. 24-30). Their prayers are filled with praising and asking. Before you ask the Lord, be sure to praise the Lord. Expect the POWER (vv. 31-37). When the church prays, we should expect things to happen. The place of prayer shook like an earthquake. It's as if God lovingly rocks the cradle of the infant church. Prayer shakes things.

PRAYER: *"Father, shake my life today as I pray."*

APRIL 7

READING: Acts 5

"And great fear came upon all the church ..." Acts 5:11

Though infant church was so surcharged with God's power a lie couldn't live there. To be a part of a Bible-believing church is a serious matter. Thus we see the POWERFUL ATMOSPHERE of the Church (vv. 1-16). Ananias and Sapphira lied and they died. There must have been some heart-searching going on inside the church and some new respect outside the church. But, there is always the UNSUCCESSFUL ATTACK upon the Church (vv. 17-32). The Jewish leaders throw the apostles in jail. The Sanhedrin gathers the next day, but they can't find the prisoners! Peters' testimony must be ours: "We ought to obey God rather than men." (v. 29). Then, there is the DOUBTTFUL ADVICE concerning the Church (vv. 33-42). At first glance, the advice of Gamaliel looks pretty good. But, we really can't be neutral when it comes to our commitment to Christ.

PRAYER: *"Lord, help me to be Your faithful, fearless, sold-out disciple today."*

APRIL 8

READING: Acts 6

" ... his face as it had been an angel." Acts 6:15

Deacon Stephen takes center stage in this thrilling account. His name means, crown. Acts 6 and 7 tell us how he came to wear the martyr's crown. Stephen is the faithful MINISTER (vv. 1-8). The church is growing. Souls are being saved. The apostles are covered up in work. But, they are to give themselves to the ministry of the Word and prayer (v. 4). Godly men must assist. Ministering to the physical needs of the people was to be their primary responsibility (vv. 2-3). Many are needed to carry on God's work. The first deacons are selected. Stephen emerges from that group. He becomes the powerful MESSENGER (vv. 9-15). Standing to speak there is something different about him. His face is glowing like an angel. The face often tells what is in the heart.

PRAYER: *"Lord, may others see the glow of Christ upon my countenance."*

APRIL 9

READING: Acts 7

"... Lord Jesus, receive my spirit" Acts 7:59

What a powerful message deacon Stephen delivers! His message is Biblical, spiritual and personal. In his message we hear what he SAYS (vv. 1-53). Stephen knows his Old Testament, giving a survey of Old Testament history. He turns to the listeners, "ye stiffnecked and uncircumcised in heart and ears, ye do always resist the Holy Ghost ..." (v. 51). People may resist God's offer of grace. After their attack on him we note what he SEES (vv. 55-56). He looks up all the way into glory. And there is Jesus, normally seated, now standing to welcome His faithful deacon home. He closes out with "Lord Jesus, receive my spirit ... lay not this sin to their charge" (vv. 59-60). Where did Stephen get that? Surely he heard about the words of Jesus on the cross (See Luke 23:34, 46).

PRAYER: *"Help me, dear Savior, to be like You in life and in death."*

APRIL 10

READING: Acts 8

"Go near and join thyself to this chariot" Acts 8:29

Who wants to leave a great city-wide crusade (vv. 1-25) and go to a desert? The Lord told deacon Phillip to do that. Often we have experiences there that can only be described as a Divine encounter. Every essential ingredient in a witnessing experience is found here. There is a Spirit Prompted SAINT (vv. 26-27a). God said, "Arise and go ..." (v. 26). And, he "arose and went!" (v. 27). Prompt obedience. He sees a Spirit-Prepared SINNER (vv. 27b-28). Riding a chariot is a responsible, religious and receptive man— the Ethiopian Eunuch. Joining himself to the chariot, Phillips uses a Spirit-Pointed SCRIPTURE (vv. 29-35). Stephen goes from Isaiah 53 directly to Jesus ("He preached unto him Jesus", v. 35). Good preaching! The result? A Spirit-Produced SALVATION (vv. 36-39). The Eunuch believes and is baptized. Desert duty may become delightful duty.

PRAYER: *"Holy Spirit, I want a Divine encounter today."*

APRIL 11

READING: Acts 9

"Who art thou, Lord? ... What wilt thou have me to do?" Acts 9:5-6

Saul (Paul) was radically saved. His conversion on the Damascus Road is still one of the greatest proofs of the reality of Christianity. Paul meets Jesus, receiving a new FAITH (vv. 1-9). He had a faith. But, now he has faith in a Person—Jesus. He asks life's two greatest questions: Who is Jesus? What does he want me to do? Paul spent the rest of his life learning the answers to those two questions. He has a new FAMILY (vv. 10-22). Those he had hated become his new family. "Brother Saul" (v. 17) must have filled his heart with joy. I'm glad I'm a part of the family of God. He has a new FUTURE (vv. 23-20). God begins to shape and prepare Paul for his future work. What a future! He has one for you.

PRAYER: *"Lord, You have saved me, now use me."*

APRIL 12

READING: Acts 10

" ... who shall tell thee words, whereby thou and all thy house shall be saved." Acts 11:14

Acts 10 is the Gentile Pentecost. Peter, a Jew, goes to the house of Cornelius, a Gentile. Calvary's River of Love is meant for the world. First, there is a GROPING CENTURION (vv.1-8). This Roman officer, Cornelius is a sincere man. He prays and is of good reputation. But, even more, he is searching for God. Second, a GROWING CHRISTIAN (vv. 9-18). Peter has a lot of growing to do. Prejudice in his heart is clogging the channels of compassion. "Not so, Lord." (v. 14). You can't call Jesus, Lord and say no, to Him in the same sentence! Third, a GATHERING CONGREGATION (vv. 19-43). Verse 33 would be any preacher's dream. Finally, a GRATIFYING CONVERSION (vv. 44-48). Before the sermon is finished, people are saved!

PRAYER: *"Help me, Lord, to rid my heart of anything that would hinder getting the Gospel to sinners."*

APRIL 13

READING: Acts 11

"And the disciples were called Christians first in Antioch" Acts 11:26

For the first time followers of Jesus are called Christians. (See Acts 26:28; 1 Peter 4:16). The enemies of Christ used it as a term of derision and scorn. God has a way of turning a scorn into a compliment! A Christian is one who belongs to Christ. The term is given to a group, not individuals. The church is called Christian because GOD is in it (vv. 19-21). The disciples pointed to God. And there is GROWTH in it (vv. 22-26). Barnabas comes, sees grace and growth, and provides guidance. There is also GIVING in it (vv. 27-30). A need is set before them and they do something. The essence of Christianity is a gift (See John 3:16). We make a living by what we get; we make a life by what we give.

PRAYER: *"Lord Christ, may I show I am a Christian by my life."*

APRIL 14

READING: Acts 12

"... but prayer was made without ceasing of the church unto God for him." Acts 12:5

James is killed. Peter is arrested. The church prays. What an intriguing chapter! Here is a triangle: a hostile world attacking; a beleaguered church praying; a prayer-answering God intervening. Consider the MYSTERY of PROVIDENCE (vv. 1-4). James is killed; Peter is delivered. Why? When we cannot trace His hand, we can trust His heart. Consider also the MINISTRY of PRAYER (v. 5). What a mighty weapon is prayer! "Without ceasing" means, stretched out. The disciples put their souls into their prayers. Finally, consider the MAJESTY of PEACE (vv. 6-16). Peter was due for execution the next morning. What is Peter doing? Sleeping! Can you imagine the faces of the disciples when Peter, in answer to their prayers, shows up at the door? We pray. And are surprised when God answers!

PRAYER: *"Lord, when I do not understand, I can lay it before Your throne of grace."*

APRIL 15

READING: Acts 13

> *"Separate me Barnabas and Saul for the work whereunto I have called them." Acts 13:2*

Now we begin the global missions section of Acts. Following Acts 1:8, the Gospel has spread from Jerusalem (Acts 1-7, to Judea/Samaria (Acts 8-12). Now, to the uttermost parts of the earth (Acts 12-28). Thus begins the first missionary journey of Paul. Arriving in Pisidian, Antioch Paul preaches a typical missionary sermon. He shares wonderful truths about salvation. He tells the people salvation is PROMISED (vv. 16-25). He brings his brief Old Testament survey to its focal point—the Lord Jesus. Then, it is PROVIDED (vv. 26-27a). God provided salvation in the crucifixion of Christ. And salvation is PRESENTED (vv. 38-41). The good news is that salvation is provided for all people everywhere! The sermon was received by some and rejected by others.

PRAYER: *"Give me a global outlook today, dear God of the nations."*

APRIL 16

READING: Acts 14

> *" ... they rehearsed all that God had done with them, and how he had opened the door of faith unto the Gentiles." Acts 14:27*

There's excitement at First Church, Antioch! Paul and Barnabas return from their first missionary journey. The place is packed. The singing is electric. The prayers are filled with praises. Now the audience is hushed as their missionaries stand to give the report of their journey. #1— JESUS was SHARED (vv. 1-20). At every stop the message was the same. That's the work of COMMMUNICATION. #2—CHURCHES were STARTED (vv. 21-25). The Great Commission says we are to make disciples, baptize and teach. How to do that? Have a church! That's the work of CONFIRMATION. #3—PEOPLE were SAVED (vv. 26-28). The missionaries don't focus on the stones, but the souls; not the bruises, but the believers! That's the work of CONVERSION.

PRAYER: *"I pray today, Lord, for those faithful missionaries who are all over the world, telling the good news of Jesus."*

APRIL 17

READING: Acts 15

"But we believe that through the grace of the Lord Jesus Christ we shall be saved, even as they" Acts 15:11

Ever try to enter a building with several doors and not know which one to use? That's what Acts 15 is all about. Paul had announced that the door of faith had been opened to the Gentiles (See Acts 14:27). That is the Jesus door. But, some said you had to enter through the Jewish door. So, there was DISSENSION (vv. 1-3). The debate must have been furious. Then there was DISCUSSION (vv. 4-18). A meeting was called at Jerusalem. Galatians gives the whole story. Peter spoke (vv. 7-11). Paul and Barnabas did (v. 12). So did James (vv. 13-18). Finally, there was DECISION (vv. 20-35). Salvation must not be through the door of DO, but through the door of DONE!

PRAYER: *"Heavenly Father, thank You that my salvation doesn't depend upon what I DO, but upon what you DID at the cross."*

APRIL 18

READING: Acts 16

"Come over into Macedonia and help us." Acts 16:9

Paul and party sail from Troas to Macedonia. The Gospel is coming to Europe! First stop—Philippi, a Roman colony. There we see three tremendous salvations. Lydia is won to Christ—a TENDER heart (vv. 14-15). The Lord opened her heart. What a beautiful picture. Jesus is the great heart specialist. She opens her home! The slave girl—a TORMENTED heart (vv. 16-21). The slave girl is on the other end of the social scale. Jesus causes the chains of spiritual slavery to fall from her soul. The Philippian Mafia, losing a source of income, kicks up the dust. Christianity always stirs up the money crowd. The jailer—a TOUGH heart (vv. 22-40). Prison preachers pray and sing. God pats His foot and causes an earthquake. In a crisis the jailer asks life's greatest question and gets the right answer (See vv. 30-31).

PRAYER: *"Lord Jesus, save some more!"*

APRIL 19

READING: Acts 17

"These that have turned the world upside down are come hither also"
Acts 17:6

Paul's enemies said that in response to his Gospel work in Thessalonica. Not really correct. Satan turns the world upside down. Jesus puts things right side up! Our churches should do that. Paul shows us how. First, we must EXEMPLIFY the SAVIOR (vv. 1-2). Jesus went to church on the Sabbath day. We follow His example on the Lord's Day. Then, we must EXPOUND the SCRIPTURES (vv. 2b-3). Bible preaching in a city has a powerful effect. And the preaching must not be just with words, but with Holy Spirit power (See 1 Thessalonians 1:5-6). And, we must EXTEND the SALVATION (v. 3c). "This Jesus, whom I preach unto you, is Christ." There it is again. The old, old story of Jesus and His love. That will turn things right side up!

PRAYER: "Lord Jesus, help me turn things right side up in my community."

APRIL 20

READING: Acts 18

"Be not afraid, but speak, and hold not thy peace." Acts 18:9

Have you ever felt like quitting? Paul evidently did when he got to Corinth. There seemed to have been a number of reasons for it reflected in 1 Corinthians 2:3. He was experiencing FATIGUE ("weakness"), FEAR ("in fear"), and FRUSTRATION ("in much trembling"). But, in the night-time the Lord gave him three promises that said, It is too soon to quit! There is the promise of His PRESENCE ("I am with thee" v.10a). Others may abandon you. Jesus never will! Then the promise of His PROTECTION ("no man shall set on thee to hurt thee" verse 10b). You are immortal until God's work in and through you is done. And, there is the promise of His POTENTIAL ("I have much people in this city" verse 10c). Jesus sees something Paul can't—people in Corinth who could be and would be saved. Too soon to quit!

PRAYER "Lord, today, help me not to quit."

APRIL 21

READING: Acts 19

"Have ye received the Holy Ghost since you believed?" Acts 19:2

A better translation is, "Did you receive the Holy Spirit when you believed?" Paul asks the question because he detects something missing in the Ephesian disciples. This lack highlights a SPIRITUAL COMPLICATION (vv. 1-4). There seemed to be no evidence of a real spiritual life among this group of professing believers. The same is a real problem today. Too many professors don't seem to be possessors. If salvation doesn't change one's life, what's the point? But, there is a SUPERNATURAL TRANSFORMATION (vv. 5-7). Now they believe ON Him (v. 4), not just about Him. Keep in mind there is a change of dispensation taking place in Acts. The experience of these Ephesians is not normative for today. The result is a SPECIAL PROCLAMATION (vv. 8-10). The inevitable result of Holy Spirit power working in believers is bold witnessing.

PRAYER: "Lord, I need Holy Spirit power to witness for You today."

APRIL 22

READING: Acts 20

"I ... have taught you publicly and from house to house." Acts 20:20

Paul's speech to the Miletus elders is one of the most moving and heartwarming in literature. He shares how he got the Gospel to the people of Ephesus. First, his MANNER (vv. 18-19). For three years he labored there. Though the work was difficult, he stayed with it. How important is faithfulness! He also served with "humility and tears." He put his heart into his work. And, he was also determined to tell the whole truth of the Gospel. He "kept back nothing ..." Second, his METHOD (v. 20). "... publicly and from house to house." God does have methods. Though times change and culture varies, public proclamation and private visitation are principles God blesses in any age. Finally, his MESSAGE (v. 21). "... repentance ... faith ..." The message is unchanging: Turn from sin! Trust in the Savior!

PRAYER: "Help me, Lord, to use God-honoring methods to get to the lost the God-originated message."

APRIL 23

READING: Acts 21

" ... the will of the Lord be done." Acts 21:14

Paul's friends seemed to say this in resignation to his insistence he would go to Jerusalem. Paul was convinced God's will for him was to go to Jerusalem, though the forecasts were foreboding. In this exchange we learn vital truths about how to know the will of God for our life. First, there is RECOGNITION. Paul and his friends all understand God does have a plan for our life. And, it is always right (Romans 12:2). Paul demonstrates RESOLUTION. Whatever the cost (v. 13) he wants God's will done in his life. "I am ready ..." What glorious determination to do God's will, regardless. Then, there will be REVELATION. Remember that God's will for our life will never contradict His Word. As we pursue God's plan for our life and surrender to it, God reveals to us what it is!

PRAYER: *"Lord, may Your will be done in my life today."*

APRIL 24

READING: Acts 22

" ... hear ye my defense ..." Acts 22:1

A changed life argues powerfully for Christian reality. Paul arrives in Jerusalem and immediately finds himself in the midst of turmoil. The arresting officer allows him to speak. He begins by saying, "Hear my defense." The word means apology. The speech he gives is a powerful argument for the reality of the Christian faith. His personal experience with Christ changed HIMSELF (vv. 3-5). He tells about pre-salvation Saul and post-salvation Paul. His experience changed his relationship to the SAVIOR (vv. 6-14). He never tired of telling about his salvation day on the Damascus Road. Then, his experience with Christ changed his experience with SOCIETY (vv. 15-21). Before he met Christ he loathed all men (1 Thessalonians 2:15). After he met Christ he loved all men (Acts 22:15). The love of Christ in him caused him to want to witness to all people. What a difference Jesus makes!

PRAYER: *"Thank You, Lord Jesus, for changing my life."*

APRIL 25

READING: Acts 23

"Be of good cheer, Paul ..." Acts 23:11

For the first time Paul is called "the prisoner" (v. 18). So, how could he be of good cheer in those circumstances? This chapter is the graphic account of God's providential dealing in the life of one willing to go to prison for Jesus' sake. Such treatment would tend to depression and discouragment. Ah, but in the night-time, Jesus gave him great encouragments. The Lord STOOD by him (v. 11). Good to know that in every crisis the Lord will stand by us. The Lord SPOKE to him (v. 11). God does speak to us. Today, He speaks to us through His Word. Words of cheer, commendation, and certainty. The Lord SAFEGUARDED him (vv.12ff). Through the rest of the chapter we read the thrilling way God providentially, preferentially, and powerfully took care of him.

PRAYER: *"Thank You, O Savior, You are with me in my night times."*

APRIL 26

READING: Acts 24

"And as he reasoned of righteousness, temperance, and judgment to come, Felix trembled ..." Acts 24:25

What a dramatic scene. Governor Felix enters with Druscilla. Paul stands before them. Paul enters in chains. What a contrast! Though freed outwardly, Felix has chains on his soul. Paul, though chained outwardly, is free in his soul. Paul faithfully preaches faith in Christ. He tells Felix about a RIGHTEOUSNESS he does not POSSESS. The rightness of God; the wrongness of man; the rightness of Christ. He tells Felix about a TEMPERANCE he does not PRACTICE. How appropriate to the audience! Felix stole his own brother's wife! Then the thunder claps. He tells Felix about a JUDGMENT TO COME for which he is not PREPARED. Down the road of life is death and judgment (Hebrews 9:27). No wonder Felix trembled. But, did he turn?

PRAYER: *"Lord, though it may not be popular, help me to tell the truth about people's need of a Savior."*

APRIL 27

READING: Acts 25

" ... unto Caesar shalt thou go." Acts 25:12

Acts 25 is preliminary to Paul's appearance before Herod Agrippa in Acts 26. First, we see Paul and FESTUS (vv. 1-12). Paul seems rather weary of the machinations of corrupt politician Festus. We read of Festus' dealings with the PLOTTERS (vv. 1-5). Jewish leaders plan to kill Paul en route to Jerusalem. To his credit, Festus declines, stating Paul will remain in Caesarea. His dealings with the PRISONER (vv. 6-12) are less honorable. Godless politicians always look for ways to get themselves out of unpleasant circumstances in a way that will save their hides! Second, we see Paul and AGRIPPA (vv 13-27). He receives some INFORMATION about Paul (vv. 13-22). Felix reviews the details of the case and Paul's appeal to Caesar. The chapter closes with the INTRODUCTION of Paul to Agrippa (vv. 23-27). There really wasn't much to send on to Caesar in the way of accusation. Truth has never been crucial to many.

PRAYER: *"Lord, even when I am treated unfairly, help me to know You are still in control."*

APRIL 28

READING: Acts 26

"Almost thou persuadest me to be a christian." Acts 26:28

Three men in our Scripture passage today illustrate the variety of attitudes toward Jesus Christ. Festus represents those who are ALIENATED from Christ (v. 24). He mistook earnestness for insanity. Paul represents those who are ALTOGETHER for Christ (vv. 2-23). He lived his philosophy of life, "To me to live is Christ" (Philippians 1:21). Agrippa represents those who are ALMOST to Christ (v. 28). Most translations indicate Agrippa was asking a derisive question. Whatever, he had heard the Gospel from the great preacher, Paul. How close he was to altogether! And in Agrippa is the story of a tragedy, the tragedy of the almost. Many there are who come close to receiving Christ, but turn and walk away.

PRAYER: *"Dear Lord, help me not to be an almost Christian, but an altogether one!"*

April 29

READING: Acts 27

" ... be of good cheer: for I believe God ..." Acts 27:25

A cts 27 is a gem of literary skill and a classic on knowledge of ancient seamanship. The chapter has also been a bulwark in substantiating the accuracy of the whole book of Acts. But, the account of storm and shipwreck, danger and deliverance teaches of the voyage of life. Using this voyage as an allegory of life, we consider the WINDS: the SITUATIONS of life (v. 4). The ship of life is blown along by many kinds of winds. Then, the ANCHORS: the SECURITIES of life (v. 29). An anchor secures the ship from drifting. Our Anchor is in heaven (Hebrews 6:19-20)! Consider the CREEKS: the SIDETRACKS of life (v. 39). So easy to get off on sidetracks as you sail along. Finally, consider the BOARDS: the SURETIES of life (v. 44). Though floating on boards, all made it safely ashore. Just like God told Paul!

PRAYER: *"Jesus, Savior, pilot me, over life's tempestuous sea."*

April 30

READING: Acts 28

" ... no man forbidding him." Acts 28:31

A cts 28 has been called the last page of the first chapter of Christian church history. Dr. Luke has now accomplished his purpose—to show the growth and progress of the infant church. Paul continues to occupy the center of the canvas. He is a PROTECTED man (vv. 1-6). Ship wreck. Snakebite. Through it all God is caring for His messenger. God's will is the safest place on earth. He is a POWERFUL man (vv. 7-10). He is a channel of blessing to others. He heals the sick. He is a PURPOSEFUL man (vv. 11-22). His great desire is to go to Rome. Mission accomplished! He is a PREACHING man (vv. 23-29). Once there he does what he always did—he preaches Jesus. So, our history of Infant's Progress closes, "no man forbidding him." One word actually, "Unhindered!" Consummation and conquest!

PRAYER: *"Thank You, Lord, that Your church continues on, and hell's gates can't prevail."*

May

RULES FOR THE ROAD.

Leviticus, Numbers, Deuteronomy?
For daily devotions? Yes, they are filled
with help as we pursue our journey
through our wilderness as did Israel
through theirs.

MAY 1

READING: Leviticus 1

" ... if any man of you bring an offering to the Lord ..." Leviticus 1:2

My early attempts to read through the Bible ended at Leviticus! It's a tough read. Why bother? Leviticus is referenced over 400 times in the New Testament. The key? Look for Jesus and you will see Him as never before. The first seven chapters talk about the Old Testament offerings. Sinners only approach God by bringing an offering. There are five in these chapters, pointing to the sacrifice of Christ on the cross. The burnt offering points to Christ's DEVOTION (1:3ff). The meal offering (2:1) to Christ's PERFECTION. The peace offering to Christ's COMMUNION (3:1). These three teach the VALUE of Christ's death. Then, the next two teach of the VICTORY of Christ's death (Leviticus 4-5). The sin offering (4:1) deals with the PRINCIPLE of sin. The trespass offering (5:6) deals with the PRACTICE of sin. Bring an offering!

PRAYER: *"O Holy Father, thank You for the one sacrifice of Christ forever!"*

MAY 2

READING: Leviticus 10

"Nadab and Abihu ... offered strange fire before the Lord ..." Leviticus 10:1

Leviticus 8-10 speaks of the priests appointed to make offerings. The prophets represented God to the people. The priests represented the people to God. Now Christ is our High Priest in heaven. On earth, we don't have a priest; we ARE priests! All is set in place. Aaron and his sons are installed (Leviticus 8) and the offerings are begun (Leviticus 9). There is a complication. Nadab and Abihu, sons of Aaron offer strange fire not commanded by God and they die. There is DESECRATION (10:1-2). Our worship cannot be careless. There are EXPLANATIONS (10:16-20). What are the lessons in this strange passage? We must worship God according to His Word. Don't trifle with holy matters. Be sure the "fire" in your worship comes from God's altar, not fires of your own making.

PRAYER: *"O holy God, may I come before You in an acceptable manner."*

MAY 3

READING: Leviticus 11

" ... ye shall therefore be holy, for I am holy." Leviticus 11:45

Leviticus 11 and 12 are strange. Clean and unclean animals. Contact with dead bodies. Birthing babies. Purity laws for the children of Israel. What's for us? The keys: "be holy, for I am holy" (11:45); "make a difference between the unclean and the clean" (11:47). The point? We must walk in purity before the Lord. There are guidelines concerning EATING (11:1-23). Calvary removed dietary restrictions (Colossians 2:16). But, eating healthy food is still wise. There are guidelines concerning TOUCHING (11:24-43). They were forbidden to touch carcasses of unclean animals. The point? Make a difference between the unclean and the clean. We must learn to distinguish between right and wrong in our life. And there are guidelines concerning BIRTHING (12:1-8). These matters of health teach the value of human life and the importance of the birth of babies.

PRAYER: *"Lord, I want to be holy as You are holy."*

MAY 4

READING: Leviticus 14

"This shall be the law of the leper in the day of his cleansing ..." ### *Leviticus 14:2*

Leprosy! What a dreaded word. The Bible uses this disease as a picture of the exceeding sinfulness of sin. First, it is a CORRUPTING DISEASE (Leviticus 14:33ff). People have no idea just how bad sin is and how devastating it can be. Sin is a problem deep within (13:2-4), isolating (13:4, 46), spreading (13:5-8), and killing (13:52,55,57). But, there can be a CLEANSING DAY (Leviticus 14:1-32). After such a gloomy, grotesque, nauseating picture of sin, it is thrilling to see how Jesus can save and cleanse from the disease of sin. A dead bird, picturing the incarnation of Christ. A living bird, picturing His resurrection and ascension. Blood shed, then sprinkled. Christ's blood shed for us is applied to our hearts (Psalm 51:7).

PRAYER: *"Lord, thank You for the cleansing blood that washes away sin!"*

MAY 5

READING: Leviticus 16

" ... to make an atonement ..." Leviticus 16:10

The Day of Atonement was the most important day of the year for the Jews. The phrase "make an atonement" is used 15 times in Leviticus 16. The word means, to cover. Each year sin was covered until Christ came. By His sacrifice at Calvary they were removed (Hebrews 10:3-12). First, the PREPARATION (vv. 2-4). One day a year the High Priest would go into the Holy of Holies and sprinkle the blood on the Mercy Seat. Christ did that for us at the cross (1 Peter 2:24). Then, the PROCEDURE (vv. 5-28). Sacrifice. Blood. Scapegoat. Jesus is sacrifice, priest and scapegoat. Our sins are gone, gone, gone! Finally, the PURPOSE (vv. 29-34). The High Priest would come out, lift his hands in blessing and cry, "You are clean from all your sins." When Jesus died on the cross, He cried, "Finished!"

PRAYER: *"Thank You, Lord Jesus, for Your atonement."*

MAY 6

READING: Leviticus 18

" ... ye shall not do ... ye shall do ..." Leviticus 18:3-4

Who is God to tell us what do and what not to do? All through this section God says, "I am the Lord your God" (v. 2). This is God's world. He establishes the rules. Don't like them? Create your own universe and rules! As long as we breathe His air and walk on His earth, better obey His rules. God intends to help us, not to hinder us. God applies His Ten Commandments to real life situations. SEXUAL matters (18:6-30). Our sex-obsessed culture laughs at sexual purity and encourages perversion. God draws a boundary around the family and says, keep sex within that circle. LEGAL matters (19:1-37). Amazingly appropriate to today's society. PENAL matters (Leviticus 20). The seriousness of the crimes listed is indicated by the punishments. The moral principles found here still apply today.

PRAYER: *"Lord, thank You for taking pains to guard my life."*

MAY 7

READING: Leviticus 21

"They shall be holy unto their God, and not profane the name of their God" Leviticus 21:6

The priests were Old Testament leaders. They were in charge of the Tabernacle, offered sacrifices at the altar, and gave the people guidance and direction from God. Now, every believer is a priest (1 Peter 2:9; Revelation 1:6). But, there are those who lead in churches today—pastors; staff members; deacons; teachers; etc. Leadership costs! There is the price of HOLINESS (Leviticus 21:1-15). Leaders are to be separated and sanctified. The Lord sets leaders apart. In our own strength we can't live a holy life. God also called the priests to WHOLENESS (21:16-24). If there was a blemish, they couldn't serve. It's different now. God uses broken people! To be a leader costs USEFULNESS (Leviticus 22:1-33). He indicates that leaders are to carry out ministry in such a way that the Lord will be pleased.

PRAYER: *"Lord, help me to serve You today."*

MAY 8

READING: Leviticus 23:1-22

"These are the feasts of the Lord, even holy convocations ..." Leviticus 23:4

Calendars. We all live by them. The Jews had a calendar. They had an agricultural one. God also gave them a spiritual calendar. There were certain times of festival, gatherings for spiritual lessons. Today, look at some of them. Passover speaks to us of REDEMPTION (v. 5). This festival commemorated the Lamb slain and blood applied as Israel was delivered from Egypt. We start the Christian life under the blood of Christ ... Unleavened bread speaks to us of CONSECRATION (vv. 6-8). Christ is our Bread of life. We are sustained by Him. Firstfruits speaks of RESURRECTION (vv. 9-14). The firstfruits of the harvest points to our resurrected Savior. Pentecost speaks of IMPARTATION (v. 15-21). After resurrection is the coming of the Holy Spirit. Every believer has been to Calvary for pardon. Have you been to Pentecost for Holy Spirit power?

PRAYER: *"Savior, You are redemption, sustenance and power to me."*

MAY 9

READING: Leviticus 23:23-44

"And Moses declared unto the children of Israel the feasts of the Lord" Leviticus 23:44

The religious calendar of the Jews continues. The final four festival days are rich in application to us. The feast of Trumpets: EXPECTATION (vv. 23-25). Trumpets were God's communication system. They were blown to assemble the people, to signal travel to begin, and to declare war. One day the trumpet will sound and we will be caught up to meet the Lord in the air (1 Thessalonians 4:16-1). Glorious expectation! The day of atonement: REALIZATION (vv. 26-32). Beautifully did this festival speak of the work of Christ on the cross. Jesus didn't just cover sin; He put sin away (John 1:29). The Tabernacles: CELEBRATION (vv. 33-44). In booths they would remember all God had done for them in the wilderness. What rejoicing. Another time of celebration yet ahead. Celebration just ahead!

PRAYER: "Lord, help me to labor with my eyes on the skies."

MAY 10

READING: Leviticus 27

"These are the commandments, which the Lord commanded Moses for the children of Israel in mount Sinai." Leviticus 27:34

Leviticus closes with a series of chapters discussing practical issues (Leviticus 24-27). The Bible is deeply spiritual, but very practical. Every day and area of our lives are to be totally dedicated to Him. Leviticus 26-27 dramatically shifts from matters of blasphemy (Leviticus 24) and liberty (Leviticus 25) to matters of integrity. Note the repetition of "if." There is to be integrity in OBEYING (26:1-13). God rewards obedience. There are penalties for disobedience. Too many want to claim the blessings and leave the curses for someone else! Integrity in TRUSTING (26:40-46). If we will repent of our disobedience and trust God, He will bless us. Integrity in VOWING (Leviticus 27). What a strange way to close a Bible book! We show our integrity when we keep our word.

PRAYER: "Help me today, Lord, to live in integrity."

MAY 11

READING: **Numbers 9**

> *" ... whether it was by day or by night that the cloud was taken up, they journeyed." Numbers 9:21*

Numbers! Names! Why bother? If our name was in the listing, we'd probably be more interested! Numbers shows the Israelites on the move. The journey through the wilderness reminds us that we are on a pilgrimage. We may fail as did Israel. We also learn how God leads us, even in difficult times. God provided a glory cloud to guide. Today, the Holy Spirit is our guide (Romans 8:14). The cloud teaches that God's guidance is CONSCIOUS (Numbers 9:14-16). We can be aware that God is leading us. It is CONSPICIOUS (Numbers 9:17). We have God's Word to check so we can be sure of the Holy Spirit's guidance. It is CONTINUOUS (Numbers 9:18-22). Our glory cloud, the Holy Spirit will lead us every step of the way.

PRAYER: *"Guide me, O Thou Great Jehovah, pilgrim through this barren land."*

MAY 12

READING: **Numbers 10**

> *"And the sons of Aaron, the priests, shall blow with the trumpets ..." Numbers 10:8*

There were no cell phones, emails, or texts in Old Testament times. Israel did have a communication system—2 silver trumpets. Hammered silver bugle-like instruments were used. Mixed signals should not be sent (1 Corinthians 14:8). We are to send out a clear Gospel blast (1 Corinthians 14:8). The trumpets were used for ASSEMBLY (vv. 1-4). The signal was given and Israel gathered. God's people must respond to the Gospel call to gather together (Hebrews 10:25). They were used for ALARM (vv. 5-9). A long blast let Israel know there was a battle to be fought. The Gospel calls us to earnestly contend for the faith (Jude 3). And there were signals for APPOINTMENTS (v.10). Days of gladness and sadness. We must answer the Gospel call to remember the Lord at special times.

PRAYER: *"Lord, maybe today I will hear the trumpet blast announcing Your return!"*

MAY 13

READING: **Numbers 11**

> *"And when the people complained, it displeased the Lord ..."*
> *Numbers 11:1*

Israel's journey to the Promised Land has its difficulties. Their experiences at three locations are recounted (Numbers 11-12). What does this have to do with us? Read I Corinthians 10:11. Our journey to glory isn't always smooth. There will be bumps in the road. Bump #1 is COMPLAINING (11:1-3). Amazing, isn't it? God had blessed them in so many ways. They seem to be complaining about things in general. Ever get into that mood? Bump #2 is LUSTING (11:4-35). Bread from heaven wasn't good enough. God sends them quail. But, it brings them judgment. God sometimes judges by letting us have our own way. Bump #3 is CRITICIZING (12:1ff). Sometimes problems come in clusters. Moses is criticized. Aaron and Miriam are disciplined. The journey is delayed. Tarrying times may be teaching times.

PRAYER: *"Lord, teach me to not let the bumps in the road define me."*

MAY 14

READING: **Numbers 13**

> *" ... we were in our own sight as grasshoppers ..." Numbers 13:33*

Spying out Canaan is the classic lesson of the perils of unbelief (Hebrews 3:18-19). God's promises to lead them into the land of Canaan (Deuteronomy 6:23). We begin with the SPIES (13:1-25). They were to search out the land which God said, "I give ..." (13:1). But most want to walk by sight, not by faith. Some Christians taste the fruits of a life of faith, but unbelief prevails. Next is the STRIFE (13:26-14:39). The report is mixed. Minority report: Enter! Majority report: They're giants; we're grasshoppers! Something is left out of the equation: God! With God grasshoppers can give giants a rough time! The account closes with the STRUGGLE (14:40-45). Israel moves now from rebellion to presumption. Bottom line: Battles of faith aren't won by the flesh.

PRAYER: *"Help me today, Lord, to live by faith, not by the flesh."*

MAY 15

READING: Numbers 16

> *"... Depart, I pray you, from the tents of these wicked men ..."*
> *Numbers 16:26*

Trouble in the camp! After all the grumbling and complaining, there is still another issue. A revolt against God's appointed leaders (Hebrews 13:7, 17). Korah and gang challenge Moses and Aaron. The CONFRONTATION (16:1-40). They correctly understand all God's people are to be holy (16:3). They fail to understand the authority of leaders. One Bible doctrine doesn't demolish another. There is a beautiful balance of doctrine in Scripture. This awesome judgment account is a lasting reminder of the seriousness of rebellion against God's leaders (Jude 11). The CONGREGATION (16:41-50). God's judgment didn't stop the rebellion. Sin is like a fired missile—once launched, it is hard to retrieve. The CONFIRMATION (v. 17). The Lord shows who is His appointed High Priest. God's leaders aren't always right. But, they are always God's leaders.

PRAYER: "Lord, today put to death every sin that arises in my heart."

MAY 16

READING: Numbers 20

> *"... speak ye unto the rock ..." Numbers 20:8*

Problems are like bananas—they come in bunches! Moses is coming to the end of his life. One would think that our lives would get simpler as we get older. It gets harder and more complex. Numbers 20 begins and ends with funerals in Moses' family. "When it rains it pours," says Morton Salt. And in between the funerals is Moses' FAILURE (vv. 1-13). God said, "speak to the rock." Instead, Moses speaks to the people and strikes the rock! The rock points to Christ. Moses had already struck the rock (Exodus 17:5-6). Christ was once smitten on Calvary. Now we speak to Him in prayer. The chapter closes with Aaron's DEPARTURE (vv. 22-29). Moses and Aaron go to the mountain. There Aaron departs. Good news for us. We have a High Priest "who ever lives to make intercession for us" (Hebrews 7:25).

PRAYER: "Father, thank You Christ was once crucified and now lives forever!"

MAY 17

READING: **Numbers 21**

> " ... *every one that is bitten, when he looketh upon it, shall live.*"
>
> *Numbers 21:8*

The Old Testament is filled with pictures that convey spiritual messages. This account of a snake bite and a serpent on a pole teach spiritual truth for us today. First, a picture of SIN (vv. 4-6). Fiery serpents bit the people. This reminds us of the pain of sin. We live in a snake-bitten world. It reminds us of the penalty of sin. Many of the people died, vividly portraying the truth of Romans 6:23. Then a picture of the SAVIOR (vv. 7-8). A brazen serpent upon a pole? Yes. Jesus was made sin for us (2 Corinthians 5:21). Then, a picture of the SALVATION (v. 9). Look and live! Look—the human side of salvation; Live—the Divine side. And everyone who looked lived!

PRAYER: *"Lord, thank You that today any who will look in faith to Jesus will be saved."*

MAY 18

READING: **Numbers 22**

> *"And the Lord opened the mouth of the ass ..." Numbers 22:28*

Balaam and his talking donkey! R. G. Lee said he'd rather hear a donkey talk than a liberal preacher preach! What an enigmatic character is Balaam. He is mentioned three times in the New Testament (2 Peter 2:15-16; Jude 11; Revelation 2:14). He is a false prophet who is a warning to the church today. Notice what King Balak SEEKS (vv. 2-21). He wants the children of Israel cursed. So he sends for Balaam, the hireling. False prophets are always money mad. We see what the Lord SENDS (vv. 22-23). This is really quite a funny scene. A donkey, an angel and a mad preacher. God has some strange preachers! Finally, what Balaam SAYS (vv. 34-35). Though a false prophet, he could speak only the word the Lord intended—blessing for God's people, not cursing.

PRAYER: *"Lord, if You can speak through a donkey, surely today You can use me."*

MAY 19

READING: Numbers 27

> *" ... Take thee Joshua ... and lay thine hand upon him ..."*
> *Numbers 27:18*

Transitions are important. The closing chapters give Israel's transition from the old to the new generation. There are new soldiers (26:1ff), new service (28:ff) and a new shepherd (27:12-23). Who can follow Moses? Such a gifted, strong leader. God has Moses' successor waiting. Joshua! The time comes when one leader must pass the baton to the new one. Joshua is selected PRIVATELY (vv. 12-17). Moses is allowed to see the Promised Land, but not to enter. Moses couldn't lead Israel in; Joshua could. Just so, the Law keeps us out; grace brings us in. What law excludes grace includes. Joshua is selected PUBLICLY (vv. 18-23). Before the people God makes it plain that there is another Spirit-filled leader for them. It is wonderful to see how the Lord moves the mantle of leadership from one to another.

PRAYER: *"Lord, help me to love and pray for our leaders."*

MAY 20

READING: Numbers 33

> *"These are the journeys of the children of Israel ..." Numbers 33:1*

For 40 years Israel goes around in circles. Now, it is time to make their journey to their new home. Numbers 33-35 tells of their MARCHING (33:1-49). There are many verses of long, dreary places where they wandered in the wilderness. But this is more than a travel log. The chapters constitute testimony to God's providences and man's responsibility for the choices made. The journey of life has its stages and stopping places. Some are determined by our decisions; others are in God's providences. There are also here chapters of CLAIMING (33:50-ff). God is emphatic: they are to claim what He has for them. Numbers closes with a summary statement: " ... these are the commandments ..." (36:13). What do we learn? "Trust and obey, for there's no other way, to be happy in Jesus, but to trust and obey."

PRAYER: *"Lord, today I want to obey You on the journey."*

MAY 21

READING: Deuteronomy 1

"These are the words which Moses spake ..." Deuteronomy 1:1

Deuteronomy! The second law! Moses is passing off the scene. A new generation is preparing to enter the Promised Land. In a series of five sermons Moses will say, farewell, to the people. He will remind them of the dangers of forgetting. All through the book we read these words, "beware ... forget not ... remember." Deuteronomy 1 is a chapter of ORGANIZATION (vv. 7-18). Gifted people are needed to share the burden and responsibilities. Also, it is a chapter of INVESTIGATION (vv. 19-40). The account of the spies is reviewed. Thus the explanation for why only the "little ones" (v. 39) could enter in. Moses then deals with their PRESUMPTION (vv. 41-46). The results of rebellion and disobedience can take years to correct. We must remember the past. We must also look to what God will do in the future!

PRAYER: "Lord, as I face today, help me to remember and to respond!"

MAY 22

READING: Deuteronomy 4

" ... He ... brought thee out ... to bring thee in ..." Deuteronomy 4:37-38

Moses preaches to the people the crucial key to the Christian life: brought out to bring in. We have been brought out of darkness into light; out of sin into salvation. To understand all this means we must make much of God's Word. Moses says we are to HEAR God's Word (vv. 1-8). "Hearken" is used almost 100 times in Deuteronomy. Not just hearing sound waves with the ear. Listening to the Word with our heart. God's Word will keep us from sin. It will give us life. And preacher Moses says we are also to HEED God's Word (vv. 9-24). To "take heed" means we are to obey what God says to us in His Word. And in so doing God will bring us out and bring us in!

PRAYER: "Lord, thank You for giving me Your Word to teach me how to get out and to get in!"

MAY 23

READING: Deuteronomy 6

> *"And it shall be our righteousness, if we observe to do all these*
> *commandments ..." Deuteronomy 6:25*

Scripture says "To obey is better than sacrifice" (1 Samuel 15:22). Moses gives motives for obedience. He speaks first concerning LEARNING God's TRUTH (6:1-9). As Moses gives them God's "commandments, statutes and judgments" (v. 1) he also shares the benefits—long life and increase. This doesn't mean to obey God will make you live to a 100 and be rich. It does mean God will bless you with a happy, holy life. They were to pass God's truth on to their children (vv. 7-9). Parents should make the home a place where their children can be educated morally, ethically and spiritually. He also speaks of REMEMBERING God's BLESSINGS (6:10-25). "Don't forget" God's graciousness (vv. 10-12) and His righteousness (vv. 20-25). Obedience leads to loving what God loves and hating what He hates.

PRAYER: *"Help me today, Lord, to obey You."*

MAY 24

READING: Deuteronomy 11

> *" ... His miracles, and His acts, which He did ..." Deuteronomy 11:3*

Israel is preparing to enter the Promised Land. Moses is preparing them for what God has prepared for them! Sometimes the best preparation is to be reminded of what God has done for us in the past. Note the repetition, "what He did." Moses reviews the lesson of God's COMPASSION (11:1-7). God has cared for us every step of life's journey. He will in the future. Then, the lesson of God's COVENANT (11:8-25). God makes promises; we claim them. We're in covenant! There is also the lesson of God's CHASTENING (11:26-32). Obedience brings blessing. Disobedience brings cursing. As Israel was between Mt. Gerizim, the mountain of blessing and Mt. Ebal, the mountain of cursing, so we are between Mt. Calvary where Jesus died for us and Mt. Olivet, where He will return for us!

PRAYER: *"Lord, today may I be preparing myself for Your return to take me to heaven."*

MAY 25

READING: Deuteronomy 12

"Then there shall be a place ..." Deuteronomy 12:11

Once in the land Israel must know how to worship God correctly. Worship! There is nothing more important than our worship of God. There is much misunderstanding about worship. Correct worship involves the right PLACE (12:1-14). Canaan would be filled with false, vile gods. Baal, the storm god; Asherah, Baal's consort. In this day of religious pluralism we must know that one god is not as good as another. We are to worship only the Lord God. For believers today worship is not about a place; it's about a PERSON (John 4:21-24). Correct worship also involves the right PROCEDURE (12:15-32). We must be careful to follow what God has laid down in His Word about how to worship Him. When we go to our church we must remember that God places His Word as the central feature.

PRAYER *"Lord, thank You I can worship at church and everyday, wherever I am."*

MAY 26

READING: Deuteronomy 16

"Three times in a year ..." Deuteronomy 16:16

God gave Israel a unique religious calendar to remind them who they were and who the Lord is; what He had done for them and what they were to do for Him. Three times each year they were to observe these feasts. Each pointed to what Christ has done for us. Passover: REDEMPTION (16:1-8). Get the yeast out! Yeast is a symbol of evil. We must get sin out of our life. Sprinkle the blood! Jesus is our Passover Lamb (1 Corinthians 5:7). Pentecost: FORMATION (16:9-12). This feast pointed to the coming of the Holy Spirit and the formation of the church (Acts 2). Our church services should be characterized by joyful celebration. Tabernacles: JUBILATION (16:13-16). Israel celebrated God's blessings and provisions in their wilderness experience. We rejoice in the glorious coming of the Lord to take us home.

PRAYER: *"Lord, thank You that today can be one of continual rejoicing in Christ."*

MAY 27

READING: Deuteronomy 19

"Thou shalt separate three cities for thee in the midst of the land ..."
Deuteronomy 19:2

The Bible is a real book about real life. Israel had the same kind of problems we face. God gives Israel laws to control behavior in the most brutal realities of life. Killing is at the top of the list. There is a distinction made between kinds of killing. He discusses INTENTIONAL killing (19:11-21). There is killing as a pre-meditated act. Calculated, progressive hate is vividly presented here. The punishment was swift and severe. "Life for life ..." (v. 21). There was no mercy in the law.

But, ACCIDENTAL killing is also discussed (19:1-10). When the taking of life was unintentional cities of refuge were available. What a beautiful picture of Christ, our Refuge!

PRAYER: *"Lord, I live in a brutal world where human life is cheap and valued very little. Help me today to respect each human life as a special gift from God."*

MAY 28

READING: Deuteronomy 29

"The secret things belong unto the Lord ..." Deuteronomy 29:29

The word "covenant" is used seven times in this chapter. In his last message to the people Moses speaks of REMEMBERING the covenant (29:1-8). We should never tire of remembering God's love and grace for us. The best way to face the future is to recall the past. He speaks of KEEPING the covenant (29:9-15). Words like "keep ... do them ... may prosper ..." speak to us. Our obedience will affect our children and grandchildren. He warns of FORSAKING the covenant (29:16-29). To fail to keep our covenant with God brings ruin (v. 23). Deuteronomy 29:29 has special meaning to us. Some things God chooses to reveal to us. We are not to pry into God's secret things. Live for the Lord now and let Him decide if and when He will tell us the secret things.

PRAYER: *"Lord, when I can't trace Your hand, I know I can trust Your heart."*

MAY 29

READING: Deuteronomy 32

> *"And Moses spake in the ears of all the congregation of Israel the words of this song, until they were ended." Deuteronomy 31:30*

Now the preacher turns singer! God gave Moses a song to give to the people. We sing of God's GREATNESS (32:1-6). What a great God we serve! Seven times in the song God is called our "Rock." He is our shelter in the time of storm; our shadow in the blazing heat; our security in the shifting sand. That's what Jesus is to us! We sing of God's GRACE (32:7-14). What a beautiful picture of God who is like the eagle stirring our nest, teaching us maturity, catching us when we fall! We sing of God's GRACE (32:39). Though we do not ignore the grief (32:21-38), we can be glad that our Lord makes alive … heals … avenges. He is our Healer and our Victor!

PRAYER: *"Give me a song in my heart today, sweet Savior."*

MAY 30

READING: Deuteronomy 33

> *"This is the blessing, wherewith Moses the man of God blessed the children of Israel before his death." Deuteronomy 33:1*

Good-bye, Moses. God's great leader of the people is at the closing hours of his life. They will cross the Jordon without Moses. But, not without God! At times Moses' words have been strong and severe. Now, they are full of grace and mercy and blessing. He points us to God's BEAUTY (33:2-5). Again he reminds of God's character and attributes. It is so good to know we are "in His hand"(v. 3). May we also be "down at thy feet," honoring His teaching. We are also pointed to God's BLESSINGS (33:6ff). Moses piles up blessing after blessing. Let's close today with this wonderful promise: " … as thy days, so shall thy strength be." (v. 25). Daily strength for whatever we need today.

PRAYER: *"Lord, I do not know the needs of today. I do know Your strength will over-match it."*

MAY 31

READING: Deuteronomy 34

> *" ... his eye was not dim, nor his natural force abated."*
> *Deuteronomy 34:7*

As we approach our last years, we may not be able to say the eyes aren't dimmed nor strength depleted! Moses had sharp eyesight and still walked with a spring in his step. Like Moses, we are walking steadily toward the time of our departure. Did Moses write this? Many write out instructions for their funeral. Perhaps Joshua wrote it. Someone will write ours. What will it say? Moses' death notice said something about his DEATH (vv. 5-8). Moses died "according to the word of the Lord." (v. 5). Such a death will be precious to God (Psalm 116:15). His death notice also said something about his DEEDS (vv. 9-12). "There arose not a prophet ... like unto Moses ..." (v. 10). But, in the future there was One (Hebrews 3:1-6). May our deeds and death honor the Lord.

PRAYER: "Lord, whenever it may come, may my death be a testimony."

June

A STACK OF OLD LETTERS.

*Here they are: Galatians, Ephesians, Philippians,
Colossians, 1 and 2 Thessalonians. Written almost
2,000 years ago. Written by Paul to young churches in
many different places. They are old, yet so fresh it seems
they were written just yesterday. And written to our
present condition and need.*

JUNE 1

READING: Galatians 1

"Who gave Himself for our sins ..." Galatians 1:4

To write a letter (or email!) is one of the most soul-revealing things we can do. Paul's letters to individuals and to churches reveal not only his soul, but the heart of God. In many ways his letter to the Galatian believers is combative. He is counteracting a lot of Gospel pollution. But, in the course of that we read some of the most marvelous statements about Christ to be found anywhere. His statement in Galatians 1:4 beautifully sets forth the finished work of Christ for our salvation. His work was VOLUNTARY (He "gave Himself"). He laid down His life for us willingly. His work was VICARIOUS ("for our sins"). He took our place on the cross. His work was VICTORIOUS ("that He might deliver us ..."). Salvation is a rescue. Christ won the victory over Satan, sin and death. Hallelujah, what a Savior!

PRAYER: *"Lord Jesus, thank You for Your finished work at Calvary."*

JUNE 2

READING: Galatians 2

"I am crucified with Christ: nevertheless I live ..." Galatians 2:20

Here is how the Christian life is lived. By His death on the cross He paid for our sins. That's substitution. By faith in His finished work we share in the benefits of that work. That's identification. We can live the Christian life victoriously because we are identified with His CRUCIFIXION ("I am crucified with Christ ..."). When Jesus was nailed to the cross, so were we! We are now dead to the life we once lived. Our eyes, lips, ears, hands and feet are dead to sin. We must claim that by faith. We live a victorious life by our identification with His RESURRECTION ("Nevertheless I live ..."). The living Lord Jesus lives His life through us as we allow the indwelling Holy Spirit to make real in us what Christ has done for us!

PRAYER: *"Lord Jesus, I don't have to sin, so I ask You to live Your life in and through me."*

JUNE 3

READING: Galatians 3

"Having begun in the Spirit, are ye now made perfect by the flesh?"
Galatians 3:3

People have a strange fascination about the teaching that one may work for salvation. The Christian Gospel isn't spelled DO; it is spelled DONE. The Galatian believers were under the mesmerizing power of teachers who taught they could be saved by works. Paul clearly reviews what salvation is all about. It is about JUSTIFICATION (v. 2). The Christian life begins when we receive the Spirit by the hearing of faith. Salvation is something you receive, not achieve (John 1:12). It is about SANCTIFICATION (v. 3). The game plan doesn't change once saved. We can't save ourselves, and we cannot live for Jesus in our own power. We cannot rely on our own strength to meet temptation. We cannot depend on our own intellect to understand the Bible. We cannot bring ourselves to spiritual maturity in our own efforts.

PRAYER: *"Thank You, Lord Jesus, for Your great, sanctifying salvation."*

JUNE 4

READING: Galatians 4

"... we are not children of the bondwoman, but of the free" Galatians
4:31

There is a strong tendency for Christians to revert back to law as a way to live the Christian life. How easy it is to go back to the bondage of rituals and rules. Paul goes to the Old Testament to show salvation is by grace, not by works. He gives an ILLUSTRATION (vv. 22-23). Ishmael was born naturally ("after the flesh", v. 29). Isaac was born supernaturally ("by promise", v. 23). They had different origins. Ishmael was born of Abraham's own reproductive powers. Isaac was born by God's power. Paul gives an INTERPRETATION (vv. 24-29). He means by "allegory" a true story with a deeper meaning. Ishmael and Isaac teach the difference between legalism and liberty; flesh and faith. He gives an APPLICATION (vv. 30-31)—Reject the way of legalism! Receive the way of liberty!

PRAYER: *"O Lord, help me today to live as a child of promise."*

JUNE 5

READING: Galatians 5

"Walk in the Spirit ... not fulfill the lust of the flesh" Galatians 5:16

At birth we get our flesh nature. At new birth we get our spiritual nature. We don't lose the old nature. It is born with us; it will be borne by us all our lives. Verse 16 is the key to understanding victory over the flesh. We live our daily life allowing the Spirit to control. This summary statement implies a CONFLICT (vv. 17-18). Flesh and Spirit are "contrary" to each other. This causes a fierce, unrelenting warfare to go on. It also implies a CONTRAST (vv. 19-23). The vices of the flesh must not be allowed to dominate. The graces of the Spirit must grow like rich fruit in our life. It implies a CONQUEST (vv. 24-26). "Walk" in verse 25 is different from verse 16. It means to be in line with the Spirit.

PRAYER: *"Today, Lord, help me to walk in step with the Spirit."*

JUNE 6

READING: Galatians 6

"Bear ye one another's burdens ..." Galatians 6:2

Life is filled with burdens. They may be physical, emotional or spiritual. What do you do with your burdens? Some must be SHARED (vv. 2-3). The word "burdens" means weight or heaviness. Some burdens are so heavy we need others to bear them with us. A trusted, praying friend. Some burdens must be SHOULDERED (vv. 4-5). There is a different word for "burden" here. It was used for the freight of a ship or the child in a mother's womb. Some burdens are personal to you and you alone can share them. Personal sins. Death. Some burdens must be SHED. We may cast our burdens upon the Lord! God is the Great Burden Bearer (1 Peter 5:7). Sometimes He takes the burden away. Praise Him for it. If not, He will give us strength to bear it. "Sustain" means to give sufficient strength.

PRAYER: *"Heavenly Father, I bring myself and my burdens to You today."*

JUNE 7

READING: Ephesians 1

> *" ... Who hath blessed us with all spiritual blessings in heavenly places in Christ." Ephesians 1:3*

To believers living in Ephesus, the banking center of the New Testament world, Paul declares, You are rich! Many Christians don't know just how rich they are. At the beginning of this rich letter Paul wants us to know the Fountain from which our rivers of blessings flow. The SOURCE of our riches ("God ... hath blessed us ..."). We have a wealthy Father who is rich in the very things we need most (Ephesians 1:7; 2:4). The SCOPE of our riches ("with all spiritual blessings ..."). Material riches come from God. But, the true riches are spiritual in nature. They are wrapped up in Christ. The lesser is contained in the greater (Romans 8:32). The SPHERE of our riches ("in the heavenlies ..."). Our new spiritual address is where the riches may be found. Rich indeed!

PRAYER: *"Father, thank You for giving me all things in Christ."*

JUNE 8

READING: Ephesians 2

> *"For we are His workmanship ..." Ephesians 2:10*

Here is your spiritual autobiography, encompassing your past (vv. 1-3), your present (vv. 4-6, 8-9), and your future (vv. 7,10). Paul shows how we are taken from guilt through grace to glory! God has great plans for you. Verse 10 tells us his IMMEDIATE plan. "We are His workmanship ..."The word also means, poem. A saved soul is His work of art. (2 Corinthians 5:17). We show His beautiful work to those around us as we walk in good works. Verse 7 tells us his ULTIMATE plan. " ... in the ages to come ..." That means, in eternity. " ... He might show ..." That means, to point out or to display. In eternity God will show us off to an amazed universe to see what He did when He saved a soul. We will be trophies of God's amazing grace!

PRAYER: *"Oh God of the universe, help me to live like a trophy of Your grace today."*

JUNE 9

READING: Ephesians 3

"For this cause I bow my knees ..." Ephesians 3:14

As Paul wrote these words, he was in prison. His prison prayers are some of the high watermarks in his letters. You can't imprison a praying person. When we pray we are free. This prayer teaches us a lot about prayer. The HUMILITY of prayer (vv. 14-15). We do not have to bow the knee when we pray, but we are often driven to our knees. Posture of body sometimes helps to rightly relate us to God. The HEART of prayer (vv. 16-19). His prayer in 1:18 is " ... that ye may know ..." Here, that you " ... may be ..." (3:18). Walk up the four steps indicated by "that." The HALLELUJAH of prayer (3:20-21). Paul bursts into doxology. When we realize on our knees God is able to do all ... above all ... abundantly above all ... exceedingly above all ... we ask ... or think, then, Hallelujah!

PRAYER: *"Dear Lord, as I bow before You, Hallelujah!"*

JUNE 10

READING: Ephesians 4

"That ye put off ... that ye put on ..." Ephesians 4:22, 24

The Christian life is to be radically different from the unsaved life. It's the difference between the old man and the new man. It's like putting off an old garment and putting on a new one. We must put off the grave clothes and put on the grace clothes! Consider the CORRUPTION of the old man (vv. 17-22). The old man is the person we used to be. Scan the verses for a full-length portrait of what the old man is like. Not a pretty picture, is it? But, consider the CREATION of the new man (vv. 23-32). The new man is the new life we have in Christ. What a difference! Changed in attitude (v. 23) and actions (vv. 24-32). What a difference Christ makes.

PRAYER: *"Lord, I am far from what I ought to be, but praise God, I'm not what I used to be!"*

JUNE 11

READING: Ephesians 5

" ... be filled with the Spirit ..." Ephesians 5:18

God's will for us is that we be filled with the Holy Spirit. This command is IMPERATIVE. The verb suggests a continuous experience to be repeated on a daily basis. Daily seek to be filled with the Spirit's power. The command is INCLUSIVE. The verb is plural. The filling of the Spirit is not just for preachers, evangelists or missionaries. Whether a dad or mom, a parent or child, you need the Holy Spirit today. The command is also INFUSIVE. The verb "filled" was used of a hollow vessel filled up. Or, a surface, covered in every part. Or, a person, thoroughly permeated. The idea is control. To be filled with the Spirit is to turn over the controls to Him. The command is IMPRESSIVE. Follow the practical results indicated in the rest of the verses, "speaking ... singing ... submitting ..." Here are the marks of the Spirit-filled life.

PRAYER: "Lord, today I ask You to take control of my life."

JUNE 12

READING Ephesians 6

"Wherefore take unto you the whole armor of God ..." Ephesians 6:13

We are in the midst of war. Gunfire flashing. Cannons booming. Swords clashing. The great war is not physical, but spiritual. There is a spiritual warfare going on and many Christians don't even know it. The Christian life is a battleground, not a playground; a war, not a waltz. We need to understand our ADVERSARY (vv. 10-12). You have three enemies: external (the world); internal (the flesh); infernal (the devil). A full-scale picture is given of our enemy, the devil. Don't underestimate him! We need to understand our WEAPONRY (vv. 13-17). "The whole armor." Each day we must suit up for battle. These articles of armor are our weapons of defense. There is a complete arsenal made available through Christ (Romans 13:12,14). We need to understand our VICTORY (vv. 17b-20). The Word and prayer!

PRAYER: "Captain of our Salvation, I suit up for battle today."

JUNE 13

READING: Philippians 1

"For to me to live is Christ ..." Philippians 1:21

What a joyful book is Philippians! Look for the joy bell ringing throughout ("rejoice ..."). Why so much joy? Paul shares the secret of a happy life (1:21). If Christ is the center of your life, all else is periphery. Jesus becomes the beginning, the basis, the beauty, the bounty and the benediction of life. Look how PERSONAL ("to me ..."). Christianity is not just joining and attending a church. Subscribing to a creed isn't the center. Having a personal relationship with the Lord Jesus is what it is all about. How PRACTICAL ("to live ..."). All of us are involved in the business of living. Many don't live; they just exist. Everything about our life takes on a new dimension. How POSSIBLE (" ... is Christ"). The Christian life is possible because we turn over the controls to Jesus. What is life to you?

PRAYER: "Lord Jesus, help me today to find my joy in living in You."

JUNE 14

READING: Philippians 2

"Let this mind be in you ..." Philippians 2:5

Sometimes spiritual truth is best understood by illustration, rather than by explanation. "A picture is worth a 1,000 words." The call to humility is illustrated by the life of Christ. We are to have the same attitude He did. Consider His POSITION (vv. 5-6). These verses take us to eternity past. The Lord Jesus had the attributes of God. He also had the attitude of God. He did not cling to His prerogatives as God's equal. He was willing to leave His heavenly position. Cosider His CONDESCENSION (vv. 7-8). Paul takes us through the steps of Christ's descent down the ladder of humiliation. The lowest rung of the ladder was His obedience to "the death of the cross" (v. 8). Then came His EXALTATION (vv. 9-11). Here is a vital principle: the way of humiliation leads to exaltation. The way down is the way up!

PRAYER: "Lord Jesus, may I today have Your attitude of humility."

JUNE 15

READING: Philippians 3

"That I may know Him ..." Philippians 3:10

Sometimes meeting a person changes one's life. When Paul asked on the Damascus Road, "Who are you?" and he heard, "I am Jesus," his life changed. Paul knows Jesus; He wants to know Him on a deeper level. Getting to know Jesus better brings POWER into your life (" ... the power of His resurrection ..."). The greatest demonstration of power this world has ever seen was when Jesus was raised from the dead. That same resurrection power is available to you! To know Him better brings PAIN into your life (" ... the fellowship of His sufferings ..."). When we know Jesus better we suffer for the things He did. To know Him brings PURPOSE into your life (" ... being made conformable unto His death"). His initial purpose is that we might die with Him in service to others. His eventual purpose is our future resurrection from death (v. 11).

PRAYER: "Lord Jesus, today I want to know You better."

JUNE 16

READING: Philippians 4

"Be careful for nothing; but in everything by prayer ..." Philippians 4:6

A good translation here is, "Don't worry about anything; pray about everything." Words for worry warts! Paul shows us the steps from the wilderness of worry to the palace of peace. Step one: PRAISE ("Rejoice in the Lord ..." v. 4). That little joy bell is stilling ringing. Rejoice in all seasons ("alway") and in all situations ("again"). Step two: POISE ("Let your moderation be known ..." v. 5). Sweet graciousness is meant. How? "The Lord is at hand" (v. 5). Either the nearness of His return or His nearness to us now has a great calming effect upon us. Step three: PRAYER (" ... in everything by prayer ..." v. 6). Too many times we have the attitude, "Why pray when we can worry?" Prayer is the step that leads us into the palace of peace (v. 7).

PRAYER: "Lord, today may I allow You to give me the peace that passes all understanding, and misunderstanding as well."

JUNE 17

READING: Colossians 1:1-14

> *" ... we ... do not cease to pray for you ..." Colossians 1:9*

Colosse! A center of heathenism and mysticism. Believers in the church there faced the same pluralistic culture we do. They needed to know they were complete in Christ and that they were the object of prayer. How good to know someone is praying for us. Prayer involves INTERCESSION (" ... to pray for you ..."). Do you pray for people by name? Prayer in general should not expect to get answers in specific. There is SUPPLICATION (" ... to desire ..."). Prayer involves making specific requests. What are you asking God for today? "The knowledge of His will" is certainly a worthy request to make of the Lord. There is APPRECIATION ("Giving thanks ..." v. 12). Thanksgiving is a big part of prayer. We ask God for what He will do. We must also thank Him for what He has done.

PRAYER: *"Lord, as I make my requests to You today, thank You for what You did for me yesterday."*

JUNE 18

READING: Colossians 1:15-29

> *" ... in Him should all fullness dwell." Colossians 1:19*

Our pluralistic culture would have us believe Jesus Christ is just one among many. We will have none of it. The Lord Jesus is the One and Only!— ABOVE the CREATION(vv. 15-17). The Creator of the universe is none other than Christ. We see His person ("image") and power ("firstborn," meaning superior in position) when we consider creation. He holds the universe together ("consist," to hold together). OVER the CHURCH (v. 18). He is the head of the church. The church is not a monarchy, ruled by the pastor; nor an oligarchy, ruled by a few; nor a democracy, ruled by the people. It is a Christocracy, governed by Christ, the head. ON the CROSS (v. 20). With one sweep of the pen we go from creation to the cross; from eternity to Calvary. God on a cross! What a picture.

PRAYER: *"Eternal Christ, how good to know You are with me today."*

JUNE 19

READING: Colossians 2

"For in Him dwelleth all the fullness of the Godhead bodily."
Colossians 2:9

Agains the background of proposed substitutes for Christ Colossians 2 sets forth the sufficiency of Christ. His DEITY (" ... all the fullness ..."). God has given a full and complete expression of Himself bodily in the Person of Christ. Christ was, is and ever will be God. His HUMANITY (" ... bodily"). Christ is God. When He came to earth, He was also man. That means He understands us. He knows what life is life. His AUTHORITY (" ... the head ..." v. 10). He is the source of all things. He has the answers to life's basic questions: Where did I come from? Why am I here? Where am I going? And, good news, " ... ye are complete in Him ..." v. 10. He satisfies every need of our life. Possessing Him, we possess all.

PRAYER: "Lord Jesus, thank You that I may find in You today all I am longing for and looking for."

JUNE 20

READING: Colossians 3

" ... Christ, Who is our life ..." Colossians 3:4

Life is what you are alive to. For some, it's family. For others, it's sports. What are you alive to? For a believer, Christ must be our life. The Christian life is a RESURRECTED life (vv. 1-2). "Since" is better than "if." It is a fact that in Christ we are identified with His death, burial and resurrection (Romans 6:3-5). We should live as people made alive in Christ. It is also a PROTECTED life (v. 3). Hidden with Christ in God. Sounds pretty safe to me! When you come to Christ you are not only saved, you're also secure. For Satan to get you he would have to get through Christ and God. It is an EXALTED life (v. 4). When Christ returns we shall appear with Him in glory. In eternity who you are will become apparent to the universe.

PRAYER: "Lord, help me to live today as one who will co-star with Jesus in glory."

JUNE 21

READING: Colossians 4

> *"Walk in wisdom toward them that are without, redeeming the time"*
> Colossians 4:5

Our daily life should be a witnessing life. To "walk" indicates how we should conduct our daily life. It is vital in our witness to others. We should be careful of our TESTIMONY (" … in wisdom …"). A good paraphrase would be, "Use your heads as you live and work among outsiders" (The Message). Our conduct must be right before we earn the right to speak to the unsaved. Proverbs 6:13 says, "He speaketh with his feet."   Indeed we do. We should be careful of our TIME (" … redeeming the time"). Time is short. We must not let it fly by without taking the opportunities it provides. To redeem the time is a picture taken from the market place. "Buying up the time" is a good translation. We must make the most of the opportunities to be a witness for Christ.

PRAYER: "Lord, today will pass quickly. Help me to be looking for witness times."

JUNE 22

READING: 1 Thessalonians 1:1-5

> *"And ye became followers of us, and of the Lord ..."*
> 1 Thessalonians 1:6

Paul spent a brief time in Thessalonica (Acts 17:1-10). The salvation of souls and the planting of a church was a miracle of God's grace. Our First Baptist Church in Jacksonville, Florida, was known as "the miracle of downtown Jacksonville." Every church is a miracle. It is a miracle because it is CALLED (v. 1). A church is made up of those called out of the world unto God (Acts 15:14). It's a miracle! It is made up of those who have been CHANGED (vv. 2-3). Changed in relation to the past ("work of faith"); the present ("labor of love"); future ("patience of hope"). It's a miracle! It is made up of those who have been CHOSEN (vv. 4-5). Election means we are very special to God. It's a miracle!

PRAYER: "Lord, today I am aware just what a miracle happened when You saved me."

JUNE 23

READING: 1 Thessalonians 1:6-10

> *" ... in every place your faith to God-ward is spread abroad ..."*
> *1 Thessalonians 1:8*

Every church is a miracle. Every saved life is a miracle as well. The believers in Thessalonica displayed the characteristics of a real Christian experience. To be saved means to be CONVERTED ("... how ye turned to God from idols ..." v. 9). To convert means to turn. Note the order: "To God from idols." When we turn to God we by necessity turn from idols. The positive comes before the negative. To be saved means to be CAPTIVATED ("to serve the living and true God"). We are not only captured by Christ, but also captivated by Him. O what a Master we have! To be saved means to be COMMITTED (" ... to wait for His Son from heaven ..." v. 10). This is the first mention of the return of Christ. Every chapter ends with a reference. We are to live looking (Titus 2:12-13).

PRAYER: "Lord Jesus, perhaps today!"

JUNE 24

READING: 1 Thessalonians 2

> *"For ye are our glory and joy." 1 Thessalonians 2:20*

This deeply personal chapter shows the pastor-heart of Paul. Things weren't always easy. Yet, he was faithful to keep sharing the Word (2:13). What kept him going? The crown of the soul-winner ahead! As he closes the chapter he sets forth his ABSENCE (v. 17). He felt like an orphaned child, so much did he miss them. He sets forth Satan's HINDRANCE (v. 18). "Satan hindered." If you are late for work today, try that one on your boss! Satan does hinder. But God can even use Satan's hindrances for His own purposes. Then he sets forth the Lord's PRESENCE (vv. 19-20). Again, he closes the chapter with a reference to the Lord's return. When Jesus returns He will have rewards for faithful service. Which one seems to motivate Paul? The soul-winner's crown. Let's live our life taking the long view.

PRAYER: "Lord Jesus, may I receive the soul-winner's crown."

JUNE 25

READING: 1 Thessalonians 3

> *" ... to comfort you concerning your faith." 1 Thessalonians 3:2*

The repetition of "your faith" is the key to what is being said here. "Your faith" is that dynamic, working principle in your life, which enables you to trust God and obey His will regardless of feelings on the inside and circumstances on the outside. Your faith needs to be INSTRUCTED (vv. 1-2). God gives us pastors to teach us the Word so as to establish and encourage us. Your faith needs to be PROTECTED (vv. 3-5). Satan seeks to shake our faith. Our faithful God will protect our faith. Your faith needs to be COMPLETED (vv. 9-13). Our faith may be "lacking," that is, have deficiencies. God will enable our faith to be made "perfect," that is brought to maturity or rendered complete. A Bible-believing local church is the best place to grow in our faith.

PRAYER: *"Lord, thank You for my church where my faith may be made strong."*

JUNE 26

READING: 1 Thessalonians 4

> *"Then we ... shall be caught up ..." 1 Thessalonians 4:17*

What is the best truth to help young converts grow? The truth that Jesus is coming again seems to have a way of maturing them. Note the four "shalls" in verses 16-17. There shall be a RETURN ("For the Lord Himself shall descend ..."). He Himself will one day return. A shout, a voice and a trumpet blast. Can you imagine? There shall be a RESURRECTION (" ... the dead in Christ shall rise first ..."). From graveyards, memorial gardens, dense jungles, sea depths believers shall rise. What a sight! There shall be a RAPTURE (" we ... shall be caught up ..."). The word, rapture, comes from the Latin word *rapio*, the translation of the verb, caught up. Living believers will be caught up and away. What a trip! There shall be a REUNION (" ... so shall we ever be with the Lord."). One huge family reunion. What a meeting! What promises!

PRAYER: *"Lord, thank You for these promises."*

JUNE 27

READING: 1 Thessalonians 5

"And the very God of peace sanctify you wholly ..."
1 Thessalonians 5:23

Sanctification is a progressive growth in righteousness believers are to experience. It is an act and a process; a position and a condition (Hebrews 10:10; 21:14). God wants us to be sanctified SPIRITUALLY ("spirit"). Our spiritual nature is our God-consciousness. The highest and most noble part of our being, we are to grow in our communion and fellowship with God. God wants us to be sanctified EMOTIONALLY ("soul"). Our emotional nature is our self-consciousness, the center of our intellect, emotions and will. Every part of our emotional being needs to grow in Christ-likeness. God wants us to be sanctified PHYSICALLY ("body"). Our physical nature is our world-consciousness. Our senses of sight, hearing, taste, touch and smell connect with the world around us. We grow in sanctification as we daily present our bodies to the Lord in total dedication (Romans 12:1).

PRAYER: *"Lord, help me to grow more like You today."*

JUNE 28

READING: 2 Thessalonians 1

"When He shall come ..." 2 Thessalonians 1:10

The focus of 1 Thessalonians is the Rapture, when Christ will catch up the saints to meet Him in the air. And 2 Thessalonians deals with Christ's return, when He will come back to earth with the saints. That return to earth is called a revelation ("When the Lord Jesus shall be revealed ..." v.7). The Lord Jesus will one day be unveiled for all to see as He makes His majestic descent form heaven. This will mean RECOMPENSE for SINNERS (vv. 8-9). "Vengeance," conveys the idea of the unwavering administration of justice. Those who reject Christ face the terrible judgment of absence from God for all eternity. His return will mean REST for SAINTS (v. 7). God's people will be a source of glory and admiration for the Lord Jesus (v. 10). The universe will see what the Lord has wrought and gasp in wonder!

PRAYER: *"Lord, may I not wait until eternity to glorify You."*

JUNE 29

READING: 2 Thessalonians 2

" ... be not soon shaken ..." 2 Thessalonians 2:2

Apostasy. The man of sin. Satanic signs and wonders. Strong delusion. That could shake one! Believers can be disturbed by a lot of unsound teaching. He writes concerning DECEPTION (vv. 2-3a). Teachers who preach and write that the church is now in the Great Tribulation can have an unsettling influence on believers. He writes concerning CORRECTION (v. 3b). He makes it very clear that the Great Tribulation ("the day of the Lord") would not come until the apostasy ends the church age and the appearance of the antichrist begins the Tribulation. He settles our hearts by writing concerning ELATION (v. 1). He starts off the chapter by telling us we need not be shaken because we can look forward to the Lord's return ("coming") and our rapture ("our gathering together unto Him"). So don't get all shook up!

PRAYER: "Lord, may I be settled by Your promises, not shaken by incorrect teaching."

JUNE 30

READING: 2 Thessalonians 3

"Now the Lord of peace Himself give you peace always by all means."
2 Thessalonians 3:16

Today we consider a calming, settling resource that will keep our hearts during such turbulent times. First, we see God's PEACE ("The Lord of peace Himself"). How desperately people need peace. There is only one place to get it. God has the monopoly on peace. It is good to know He will give it "always by all means." Whatever times you are going through and in all the varied circumstances of life we can have God's peace. Second, we see God's PRESENCE ("The Lord be with you all" v. 16). The peace of God is ours because the God of peace dwells within us (Philippians 4:7, 9). Third, there is God's PROVISION (" ... grace ... be with you all" v. 18). God gives peace because He has first given us grace! So, why be troubled?

PRAYER: "Lord God of peace and grace, thank You for giving me both."

July

HOW THE WAR WAS WON/LOST.

Joshua. Judges. Ruth. What action-packed books! The principles of spiritual victory and the problems of spiritual defeat will engage us during the days of July.

JULY 1

READING: Joshua 1

"This book of the law shall not depart out of thy mouth ..." Joshua 1:8

Israel is on the east bank of Jordan. Canaan is just across the river. Joshua illustrates what believers must understand: God has blessed us with all blessings in Christ (Ephesians 1:3). We must claim them. Joshua's assignment is helpful to us. The assignment involves national matters concerning the land (vv. 1-6). It also involves personal matters concerning the law (vv. 7-8). Israel's Bible had only five books ("the law"). We have sixty-six. The way to claim our spiritual blessings is the same. We must DECLARE the Word ("not depart out of thy mouth ..."). We must DIGEST the Word ("thou shalt meditate therein ..."). Meditation is to the soul what digestion is to the body. We must DO the Word ("that thou mayest observe to do ..."). The destination of meditation is application.

PRAYER: "Thank You for my Bible. May I read it and heed it today."

JULY 2

READING: Joshua 2

"For we have heard how the Lord dried up the water of the Red Sea for you ..." Joshua 2:10

The remarkable story of Rahab, the prostitute is before us here. She is one of the most famous converts in the Old Testament, mentioned in three New Testament chapters (Matthew 1; Hebrews 11, James 2). She tells the spies an amazing story. She shares how she, as a Canaanite prostitute, came to know the Lord. She shares about the message she HEARD (vv. 8-10). She had heard the promise (v. 9), and acknowledged the power (v. 10). She could see what the Lord had done for the Israelites. The life of a changed believer is most effective in winning the lost. She shares about the message she HEEDED (vv. 11-13). Evidently when others heard they did nothing. She heard it and believed! And it got her in the family tree of Jesus (Matthew 1:5).

PRAYER: "Thank you, Lord, that sinners can believe and be saved."

JULY 3

READING: Joshua 3

> *"Sanctify yourselves: for tomorrow the Lord will do wonders among you." Joshua 3:5*

The crossing of the Red Sea illustrates salvation. The crossing of the river Jordan illustrates sanctification. Also, it teaches us how to overcome the rivers of difficulty we face. We learn here about the WAITING of the people (vv. 1-2). For three days they waited. Why the delay? To organize and get final instructions. Sometimes the Lord puts us in a holding pattern. We may not know the reasons, but God has a plan. We also learn about the WORDS to the people (v. 3-13). What a message Joshua delivered to Israel! "Tomorrow God will do wonders." The parting of the Jordan was a miracle. A miracle is God doing what He chooses to do with His own creation. He is still in the business of parting the waters. "God any rivers you think are impossible? ..."

PRAYER: "Lord, thank You for the promise that You can handle the rivers I face today."

JULY 4

READING: Joshua 5

> *"Nay; but as Captain of the host of the Lord am I now come." Joshua 5:14*

Why are we studying today an ancient military strategy manual? Because the Old Testament book illustrates our victory in Christ. We are soldiers in the Lord's army, fighting battles against the world, the flesh and the devil. Here we find the steps to being ready. PREPARING the Lord's army (vv. 2-10). Sometimes it is painful to learn we do not win spiritual battles by anything we do in the flesh. FEEDING the Lord's army (vv.11-12). To be successful in our spiritual battles, we must be well-fed spiritually. LEADING the Lord's army (vv. 13-15). Joshua is the leader. Or, is he? Jesus, the Captain of our salvation is in charge (2 Corinthians 2:14). When the Lord is in charge, victory is assured!

PRAYER: "Today, Lord Jesus, I look to You to give me victory in the battles I face."

JULY 5

READING: Joshua 6

" ... the wall fell down flat." Joshua 6:20

Jericho looms ahead. The Jordan has been crossed. Now, the first campaign to conquer Canaan. Joshua 6 is a classic study in military science. More importantly we learn how to win the battle over the Jerichos in our life. We begin with the SIEGE (v. 1). Jericho is a picture of our spiritual enemies. We have strong cities to conquer. Some habit? The influence of bad friends? Some weakness in personality? Lay siege on it! God has promised victory. Then, the STRATEGY (vv. 2-15). Strange strategy indeed. Marching round and round the walls, blowing trumpets. God knows what He is doing (2 Corinthians 10:4). Finally, the SUCCESS (vv. 15-27). "And the walls came a tumblin' down!" You may have been around your Jericho six times. Don't give up. Victory is just ahead. The walls will come down.

PRAYER: "Lord, I have my Jerichos to face today. Help me to obey Your instructions and claim Your victory over them."

JULY 6

READING: Joshua 7

" ... Get thee up ... Israel hath sinned ..." Joshua 7:10-11

Our biggest threats come from within, not without. Jericho represents the world. Achan's sin represents the flesh. Follow this sad chapter as it unfolds. Israel's DEFEAT (vv. 2-5). God's people are never more in danger than right after a great victory. The journey from a great victory to a humiliating defeat can be a short one. What causes it? There is no mention of prayer and dependence upon God. There is great evidence of self-confidence. Ai seemed such a little place. The little things often defeat us. Joshua's DISCOVERY (vv. 6-23). In brokenness and prayer Joshua discovers the problem. There is sin in the camp. We can only expect defeat when there is sin in our life. Achan's DOOM (vv. 24-26). The concluding verses aren't pleasant reading. But, they warn we must deal with sin in our life.

PRAYER: "Lord, help me face any sin in my life today that might defeat me."

JULY 7

READING: Joshua 8

"Fear not, neither be thou dismayed: take all the people of war with thee, and arise, go up to Ai ..." Joshua 8:1

Ai may be turned from defeat to victory. It is never easy to recover lost ground in the Christian life. Thirty minutes of sin can take away thirty years of God's blessing. But victory may be had. Victory PROMISED (vv. 1-2). "Fear not, neither be thou dismayed." God spoke the same words to Moses (Deuteronomy 1:21) and Joshua (1:9). When we are afraid and discouraged we can look to the promises of God. Victory PURSUED (vv. 3-27). God's plan of victory over Ai is the opposite of the one for Jericho. God is not limited to any one plan or method to do His work. God is never boring! Victory PRESERVED (vv. 28-35). Destruction (vv. 28-29) is followed by instruction (vv. 30-35).

PRAYER: "Lord, I claim victory over the Ai's in my life."

JULY 8

READING: Joshua 9

"And Joshua made them that day hewers of wood and drawers of water ..." Joshua 9:27

We all make mistakes. What do you do when you make them? Israel's experience with the Gibeonites shows us how mistakes are made and what to do about it. Jericho represented the world. Ai represented the flesh. The Gibeonites represent the devil. We are warned of the deceptions of the devil (Ephesians 6:11). We see here how deception is DEPLOYED (vv. 4b-15). God has a battle strategy for our victory. Satan has a plan for our defeat. How it is DISCOVERED (vv. 16-19). It took just three days for Israel to discover it had been deceived. They lived with that mistake for a lifetime. And so may we. Thankfully, we learn how deception is DEFEATED (vv. 20-27). Put your mistake to work for you! God can use our mistakes to make us stronger.

PRAYER: "Lord, help me today to turn my mistakes into messages."

JULY 9

READING: Joshua 10

"But these five kings fled and hid themselves ..." Joshua 10:16

Five kings hear what Gibeon has done and they are infuriated. Let's consider the message of these five kings in our personal life. They are HIDDEN (vv. 15-21). Are there some things hidden in a cave in your life. A tongue problem? Pride? Hidden lust? From time to time they may suddenly dash out of their hiding place. You can't conquer your Canaan until you deal with the kings hidden in the cave. They are HUMBLED (vv. 22-25). "Feet upon the necks" (v. 24) signifies complete subjection of a defeated enemy. Our enemies can be under our feet because they are under Jesus' feet (Psalm 8:6). Claim victory over that pride, lust, tongue in Jesus' name! They are HANGED (vv. 26-27). The only way to get victory over hidden things in our life is to put them to death (Colossians 3:5).

PRAYER: *"Lord Jesus, thank You my sins are under Your feet."*

JULY 10

READING: Joshua 14

"Now therefore give me this mountain ..." Joshua 14:12

Joshua's old friend, Caleb, steps on the Bible stage today. He is now 85 years old. The last leg of his journey has come. Let's listen in on him. What he RECALLS (vv. 6-9). As we get older we like to reminisce. Caleb does so about his role as one of the 12 spies. He testifies to his total dedication to God (v. 8). So now he is on the verge of occupying the land God had promised. What he REQUESTS (vv. 10-12). After such a long life surely he can be excused if he retires to a quiet place. What he requests is breathtaking—Give me this mountain! Rather than gloating over past victories he is gearing up for new ones. What he RECEIVES (vv. 13-15). God gives him a place to settle (vv. 13-14) and a peace to satisfy (v. 15).

PRAYER: *"Lord, I want that mountain of opportunity just ahead."*

JULY 11

READING: Joshua 20

> *"And he shall dwell in that city ... until the death of the high priest ..."*
> *Joshua 20:6*

Four Old Testament books mention the refuge cities (Exodus 21; Numbers 35; Deuteronomy 19; here). They provide a beautiful picture of the Lord Jesus as our refuge. Consider FLEEING to the cities (vv. 3-5). If a person killed someone accidentally, they were to flee to one of the cities. The roads were kept in repair, signs were placed along the way. The cities were all on mountains and the gates were never shut. The lessons about fleeing to Christ for salvation are obvious. Consider DWELLING in the cities (v. 6). One could stay in the city until the death of the High Priest. Jesus, our High Priest, never dies, so we take refuge forever (Hebrews 7:24-25). Consider the NAMING of the cities (vv. 7-9). Each name has meaning and points to what we have in Christ.

PRAYER: "Lord Jesus, You are my Refuge."

JULY 12

READING: Joshua 23

> *"Be ye therefore very courageous to keep and to do all that is written in*
> *the book ..." Joshua 23:6*

The time has come for the old soldier to say good-bye. Joshua is 110. Time has come to go the "way of all the earth" (v. 14). What a life he has experienced. It started in Egyptian slavery. It continued with the wilderness experience. It closes with a worship service in the Promised Land! He leaves them with the prescription for spiritual victory. SEPARATION (v. 7). It is foolish to worship the gods of a defeated enemy. God expects us to be separated to Him (Romans 12:2). CONSECRATION (v. 8). "Cleave unto the Lord." What a blessing to be able to do that. DEVOTION (v. 11). "Love the Lord your God." Love for Jesus is the key to the Christian life.

PRAYER: "Lord, help me to so live today that translation into our Promised Land would be a blessed and sweet time to others."

JULY 13

READING: Judges 1

" ... but could not drive out the inhabitants of the valley ..." Judges 1:19

Joshua tells how the battle is won. Judges tells how the battle is lost. Shouts of victory turn to cries of misery. Israel's gradual compromise with Canaanite culture is a graphic picture of how believers may compromise with current culture. The process of compromise is gradual. We see Israel FIGHTING the Canaanites (vv. 1-18). There is victory at the beginning. Obeying the Word of God, prayer (v. 2) and cooperation (v. 3) bring victory. But, we next see Israel FEARING the Canaanites (vv. 19-28). The chariots of iron intimidated them. It isn't that God's people cannot drive out forces of evil. God could and would! Then we see Israel FOLLOWING the Canaanites (vv. 29-37). Cannan is now in Israel! Losing culture wars is a step-by-step process. Here a little, there a little compromise. And the battle is lost.

PRAYER: "Lord, help me today to stand firm upon God's Word."

JULY 14

READING: Judges 2

"And the children of Israel did evil in the sight of the Lord ..."
Judges 2:11

Judges 2:11-19 provide a summary of the entire book of Judges. There is a pattern repeated over and over again. It actually might be called a sin cycle. It begins with REBELLION (v. 11). They did evil in that they started serving Baal, the filthy god of Canaan. Many segments of the American church have bowed to the godless, immoral culture of the time. RETRIBUTION (vv. 14-15). God is a God of love, but also a God of wrath. His holy character must deal with sin. REPENTANCE (v. 15). We learn from other passages that Israel would repent. Repentance brings God's forgiveness. RESTORATION (vv. 16-19). God would raise up Judges who would be used to deliver God's people. This sin-repentance cycle led downward to degeneration. The sin cycle is operating today.

PRAYER: "Lord, help me to break the sin cycle in my life."

JULY 15

READING: Judges 3

>   *"And when the children of Israel cried unto the Lord, the Lord raised up*
>   *a deliverer ..." Judges 3:9*

When Israel fell into judgment God raised up Judges to deliver them. They were just ordinary people. Many of them were limited in their capabilities and had problems in their lives. But, God can hit straight licks with crooked sticks! Othniel teaches us the lesson of EXPERIENCING God's PRESENCE (vv. 5-11). Othniel was ordinary; what made him a leader? "The Spirit of the Lord came upon him..." (v. 10). Ehud teaches the lessons of EXECUTING God's PLAN (vv. 12-130). Some think he had a handicap. God will use us in spite of physical problems or emotional scars. Shamgar teaches the lessons of EXPECTING God's POWER (v. 31). He's only a blip on the screen. God put an unusual tool in his hand. And God used him to show His power!

PRAYER: *"Lord, I know I am ordinary. Use me in extra-ordinary ways."*

JULY 16

READING: Judges 4

>   *"And Deborah, a prophetess ... judged Israel at that time." Judges 4:4*

Now, Israel's Margaret Thatcher steps on the national stage. Whatever your view of the role of women in church or society at large, it is clear that God elevates women to special places of usefulness. Thank God for the Deborah's among us! Look at this remarkably gifted woman's RESUME (vv. 4-5). As a prophetess she received revelation from God. As a judge she rendered national decisions. She was Israel's political, judicial and spiritual nerve center. Look at her REVELATION (vv. 6-7). God says here, you draw; I will draw. What a promise of victory! Look at her ROLE (vv. 8-9). Was Barak a coward? No. Barak had enough sense to know he needed the help of this godly woman. Leaders in our churches need the prayers and help of the godly women in their midst. Thank God for the Deborah's.

PRAYER: *"Lord, bless the faithful women in the work of the Lord."*

JULY 17

READING: Judges 6

"The Lord is with thee, thou mighty man of valour." Judges 6:12

Gideon heads the list of Judges in Hebrews 11:32. He is the best known of the Judges. We learn a lot about Gideon and God today. His COMMISSION (vv. 11-24). "Mighty man of valour." Gideon must have looked around. Who me? Yes, God was going to make him just that. God sees you as you can be, and what He can make of you. His COURAGE (vv. 25-35). Gideon shows his allegiance to the Lord by tearing down the altars of Baal. God may use you to tear down some altars of sin. His CAUTION (vv. 36-40). He wants God to be with him. He puts out the fleece. This is not the best method. He already has the promise of God's Word. God does sometimes come down to our level of weakness. Jesus did for Thomas.

PRAYER: "Lord, I don't need a fleece. I have Your Word."

JULY 18

READING: Judges 7

"The people that are with thee are too many ..." Judges 7:2

It is amazing what God can do with a few. Or you! Follow this thrilling account and you will see. REDUCING the Army (vv. 1-8). Gideon's army is reduced from 32,000 to 300. The Midianites number 135,000. God sometimes cuts down our resources so we will depend more on Him. ASSURING the General (vv. 9-15). The Lord again assures Gideon of the victory. When he heard the enemy announcing defeat he just "worshipped" (v. 15). Victory is on the way! DEFEATING the Enemy (vv. 16-24). Stand where you ought to stand (v. 21). Use God's tools for victory. Blow the trumpets, smash the pots, lift the torches and shout, "The sword of the Lord and of Gideon" (v. 20)! God doesn't have to have large numbers to do His work and win the battles in your world.

PRAYER: "Lord, thank You that today You can win the victory by just a few."

JULY 19

READING: Judges 8

> *"And Gideon made an ephod ... which thing became a snare unto Gideon, and to his house." Judges 8:27*

So far Gideon is a victorious hero. But, one evidence the Bible is inspired is that it tells the truth about its heroes. We desire to finish well. Gideon faces a series of hurdles. #1: CRITICISM (vv. 1-3). How does Gideon respond to criticism? He places the unity of God's people above his personal hurts. He can control an army. He can also control himself. #2: CONTEMPT (vv. 4-21). God's own people don't support him. If you are serving the Lord for any other reason than Jesus' sake, you are destined to become a bitter old person. #3: COMPROMISE (vv. 22-35). That one got him. The day Gideon puts on the ephod of his own making, he and Israel are on the way down. Don't come to life's last hurdle and stumble. Never compromise God's Word.

PRAYER: "Lord, help me to finish well."

JULY 20

READING: Judges 9

> *"Then said all the trees unto the bramble, 'Come thou, and reign over us'." Judges 9:4*

Judges 9 is filled with blood. Yet, it is very revealing about the spiritual, moral, and political state of Israel. And ours as well. This lengthy chapter highlights Abimelech, a corrupt politician. INAUGURATION (vv. 1-6). He's quite ambitious, isn't he? He decides to be king, whatever it takes. He raises support (v. 4), gets some experts (v. 4), and eliminates competitors (v. 5). Sound familiar? REPUDIATION (vv. 7-21). His brother, Jotham, escapes and messes up the inauguration. His yell from the hill is a parable of the trees. Mr. Bramble, the most worthless of all, has been selected to be the leader. The parable is a prophecy of future disaster. When the unfit are chosen to lead, trouble is ahead. DISINTEGRATION (vv. 22-57). Not a pretty conclusion. Destruction and death await poor leadership. Is judgment near for America?

PRAYER: "Lord, today may godly people become our leaders."

JULY 21

READING: Judges 11

> *"... Jephthah ... was a mighty man of valour ... the son of an harlot ..."*
> *Judges 11:1*

Jephthah could be called a leader from the wrong side of the tracks. How many leaders have started from lowly status and were elevated to places of great leadership. Consider his DIFFICULT PAST (vv. 1-11). You don't have to be a captive to your past. God can and will use you. His DEFINITE POWER (vv. 12-29, 32-33). The secret of Jephthah's power is found in this statement, "Then the Spirit of the Lord came upon Jephthah ..." (v. 29). This will be the secret of our power also. His DECISIVE PROMISE (vv. 30-31, 34-40). This puzzling conclusion teaches many lessons. One is, we are certainly not bound to keep foolish vows. Another is, we should keep those vows we make to follow and serve the Lord.

PRAYER: *"Lord, I know You can use me and I make a vow today to surrender to Your will."*

JULY 22

READING: Judges 13

> *"... Samson ... grew, and the Lord blessed him." Judges 13:24*

How often have we heard of Samson. There is more about him in Judges than any other leader. You would have liked Samson. His name means, sunny. He was handsome, athletic, joke-telling and fun-loving. Yet, he is one of the Bible's great tragedies. He is promising in his CONCEPTION (vv. 1-12). His godly parents dedicated him to the Lord. He is to be a Nazarite, one totally separated to the Lord. His CHILDHOOD (vv. 24). What sunshine he must have brought into his home. He grows under the careful guidance of his parents. He shows evidence of God's grace ("The Lord blessed him"). Is your home-life godly? You have a head start in life. His CHARISMA (v. 25). Four of the seven references to the Holy Spirit in Judges are connected with Samson. Is the Holy Spirit working in your life today?

PRAYER: *"Holy Spirit, I yield my life to You today."*

JULY 23

READING: Judges 14

"Get her for me; for she pleaseth me well." Judges 14:3

Samson probably had more potential than any other person in the Old Testament. Yet, this superboy becomes a playboy. His life is an enigma. He squandered God's resources in his life. Judges 14-15 traces the steps downward in his life. Samson STRAYS from God (14:1-20). Carnal desire; parental disrespect; spiritual defilement; personal disgrace. All because he wanted what looked good to him. He STANDS for God (15:1-17). Chapter 15 begins with some victories, but ends with a prayer of desperation. The Holy Spirit is still at work in his life. Samson STRUGGLES with God (15:18-20). He makes his appeal to God for water. He seemed to have spiritual yearnings as well as physical ones. But, the physical overcomes the spiritual.

PRAYER: *"O God, help me not think that just because my physical needs are met today that I have no need of spiritual blessings."*

JULY 24

READING: Judges 16

"Howbeit the hair of his head began to grow again ..." Judges 16:22

Samson could conquer his enemies on the outside, but not his enemies inside. He is the classic illustration of 1 Corinthians 10:12, "Wherefore let him that thinketh he standeth take heed lest he fall." Samson's FOLLY (vv. 1-19). He foolishly thinks you can play the sin game and not be harmed. Delilah's lap is dangerous! Samson's FALL (vv. 20-21). Everything suddenly collapses. From here on out he loses—his hair; strength; eyes; liberty; testimony. You always lose in the sin game. "He wist not that the Lord was departed from him." (v. 20). One of the saddest verses in the Bible. Look at the blinding, binding, grinding results of sin (v. 21). Samson's FORGIVENESS (vv. 22-31). Samson repents and is restored spiritually. Restored hair becomes a visible sign of recovery.

PRAYER: *"Lord, I have failed You in many ways. Thank You the hair can grow again."*

JULY 25

READING: Judges 18

"In those days there was no king in Israel ..." Judges 18:1

The key to Judges is found in Judges 17:6. To the statement about no king is added these words, " ... but every man did that which was right in his own eyes." When a people do what is right in their eyes rather than in God's, social insanity won't be far off. Judges 18 is like reading the daily newspaper. COVETOUSNESS (vv. 1-10). The Danites couldn't be satisfied with what they had. They wanted what others had. Advertising constantly appeals to our coveteous spirit. VICIOUSNESS (vv. 11-26). Here's what happens when people are free to choose their own lifestyle. Too often the choice leads to incest, sexual molestation, rape and murder. BLOOD-THIRSTINESS (vv. 27-31). The philosophy here is, "What's yours is mine, and I'll take it." The only way out is to return to what is right in God's eyes.

PRAYER: *"Lord, today may I be guided by Your standards, not mine."*

JULY 26

READING: Judges 21

" ... no king ... right in his own eyes." Judges 21:25

Judges closes with the key hanging on the back door. Israel is man-centered not God-centered. This is the essence of humanism. Humanism says man is the solution to his own problems. The last two chapters of Judges (20-21) show us the painful price of humanism. Chapter 20 tells us the price of NATIONAL DISRUPTION. What we read about is a civil war. It shows God's judgment on a sinning nation. The social ills we face as a nation aren't the reasons for judgment; they are the result of judgment. Chapter 21 tells us the price of MARITAL CONFUSION. The message here is that sin not only hurts national life. Sin also creates the pain of domestic devastation. The book ends. Is there no hope? Don't stop now. Tomorrow's devotion will give hope. READ THE NEXT BOOK!

PRAYER: *"Lord, things look dark in our nation and in our homes. I eagerly await hope."*

JULY 27

READING: Ruth 1

" ... and they came to Bethlehem ..." Ruth 1:22

Ruth is like a shining pearl after the pig-pen of Judges. In the midst of darkest days there are some bright spots. Ruth abounds in beautiful spiritual lessons. A love story that culminates with the birth of a baby in Bethlehem. How God works in the lives of people. We see here A DISTURBED FAMILY (vv. 1-5). This family of believers lets the famine drive them to Moab. Instead of staying in the house of bread (Bethlehem) and trusting God they go to the wash pot (Psalms 60:8). They find funerals. Then we see A DECIDED FUTURE (vv. 6-14). Orphah goes backward. Ruth goes onward with Naomi. She's heard enough of the true God to want to know Him. Then, A DECLARED FAITH (vv. 16-22). Beautiful words expressing faith and deciding destiny. The chapter closes with a girl, a village and God.

PRAYER: "Lord, help me today to move toward God's Bethlehem."

JULY 28

READING: Ruth 2

"Why have I found grace in thine eyes ..." Ruth 2:10

No surprise why Ruth found grace in Boaz's eyes—she was good looking! Ruth learns the meaning of grace. EXPECTING Grace (vv. 1-3). Naomi sends Ruth to the fields of Boaz. She is a foreigner. She is hoping to have someone be gracious to her. Enter Boaz. EXPERIENCING Grace (vv. 4-16). Boaz sees Ruth and extends grace to her. Her question to Boaz is ours to the Lord. We don't deserve grace. But, God's grace is extended to us, not because of anything in us, but everything in Him! EXPRESSING Grace (vv. 17-23). When we experience grace we must express it. Ruth does with her lips (vv. 17-21) and her labor (vv. 22-23). When we have experienced God's grace we should share it with our lips and show it with our service.

PRAYER: "O God of grace, I am unworthy of what You have freely given me in Christ."

JULY 29

READING: Ruth 3

> *"For the man will not rest until he have finished the thing this day."*
> *Ruth 3:18*

Ruth places herself at the feet of her Bethlehem redeemer. How she was redeemed by Boaz illustrates how we come to Christ. PREPARATION for the Redeemer (vv. 1-5). Naomi turns Ruth's attention to Boaz. Those of us in the family of God need to point others to Christ. She is to place herself at Boaz's feet. PRESENTATION to the Redeemer(vv. 6-13). She is following the established procedures of that day. She is requesting redemption. Her request is good news to Boaz. He loves her dearly. Salvation is not just a legal transaction. It is a love affair. PROCLAMATION about the Redeemer (vv. 14-18). Boaz gives Ruth blessings to share with others. If you spend time at Jesus' feet, you have something to share with others.

PRAYER: "Lord Jesus, thank You for loving me enough to redeem me with Your precious blood."

JULY 30

READING: Ruth 4

> *"... that his name may be famous in Bethlehem." Ruth 4:14*

Today we are going to a wedding! Ruth will marry Boaz. She is in his heart. Now she will be in his home. He will redeem her and make her his bride. In Boaz's actions we observe some ARRANGEMENTS (vv. 1-18). Notice that Boaz makes all the arrangements. Salvation is God's great work. He skillfully removes the other redeemer! There are some ANNOUNCEMENTS (vv. 9-12). He redeems her property and her person. "Famous in Bethlehem." Bethlehem is the birthplace of the Lord Jesus. And Ruth will be included! There are some ACCOMPLISHMENTS (vv. 13-17). Ruth is in the family. She has been brought in because Boaz loved her. When we come to Jesus we become part of God's family. Redemption here results in a wedding and the birth of a baby. Don't overlook the genealogy. It makes a connection to your New Testament.

PRAYER: "Lord Jesus, thank You for coming to Bethlehem and into my heart."

JULY 31

" ... and Boaz begat Obed of Ruth ..." Matthew 1:5

READING: Matthew 1

The book of Ruth ends with a genealogy. Matthew's Gospel begins with one. Ruth is mentioned in both. It is most unusual for a Jewish genealogy to include a woman. Let's look at three today. They tell us the way to get into the family of Jesus. THAMAR (1:3) got in because she was a SINNER. She deserved stoning, according to the law. We deserve hell. But, Jesus includes us by grace. RAHAB (1:5) got in because she was a BELIEVER. This harlot heard the story of what God could do, believed it and was saved. Belief in Jesus gets us in the family (Acts 16:31). RUTH (1:5) got in because she was a RECEIVER. She was excluded by law, but included by grace. And so are we!

PRAYER: "Lord Jesus, thank You for allowing me, a sinner, into Your family."

August

THE CORINTHIAN CORRESPONDENCE.

*Paul started the church at Corinth on his
second missionary journey. But not all was well.
Problems emerge. He writes two letters to deal with
the problems and encourage them. In our daily
devotions this month let's learn from this troubled,
triumphant church.*

AUGUST 1

READING: 1 Corinthians 1

"That no flesh should glory in His sight." 1 Corinthians 1:29

A survey of the membership at Corinth church wouldn't highlight many high and noble. Rather, the church was composed of a bunch of so-called nobodies. God seems to specialize in using people this world would never have chosen. God's nobodies are SELECTED by Him (vv. 26-29). Paul doesn't mean there aren't ANY of noble birth that God uses. Just not "many." If God used you because of who you are, you would be hard to live with in heaven! God's nobodies are LOCATED in Him (vv. 30-31). Capability for service is not based on who we are, but who He is! He is our "righteousness," to cover our past; our "sanctification," to cope with our present; our "redemption," to care for our future. So, if you feel like a nobody, congratulations. You're just the kind of person God can use.

PRAYER: "Lord, I feel my own inadequacy. Use me."

AUGUST 2

READING: 1 Corinthians 2

"But we speak the wisdom of God in a mystery ..." 1 Corinthians 2:7

The Corinthian church was having problems because she was enamored with man's wisdom, and failed to see the simplicity of God's wisdom. God's wisdom can be comprehended because the Holy Spirit reveals it (vv. 9-13). God's wisdom. We get God's wisdom by spiritual REVELATION (vv. 9-10). God has chosen to reveal Himself to man. At salvation His Spirit comes to dwell in our hearts. The Holy Spirit alone can make the things of God known to us. This is not something you achieve; it is something you receive. By spiritual ILLUMINATION (vv. 11-12). The Holy Spirit must illuminate our understanding as we study the wisdom of God in His Word. By spiritual INSPIRATION (vv. 13). The Holy Spirit always speaks in the context of the Bible. The Spirit of God never contradicts the Word of God.

PRAYER: "O Holy Spirit, open my spiritual eyes that I may see."

AUGUST 3

READING: 1 Corinthians 3

" ... ye are God's building." 1 Corinthians 3:9

Paul expands the picture of the church as a building. We must be aware we are building for eternity. Paul mentions several aspects. The FOUNDATION (vv. 10-11). There is no doubt that the church and the Christian life must be built upon a foundational experience with Jesus Christ. He alone is the right foundation. There can be no Christian life until there is a Christian experience. One cannot build a skyscraper on a chicken coop foundation. "On Christ the solid rock I stand ..." The CONSTRUCTION (vv. 12). Each day we have a choice of materials to use to build for eternity. "Wood, hay, stubble." Perishable materials from the devil's lumber yard. "Gold, silver, precious stones." Permanent materials from the King's treasure house. The EXAMINATION (vv. 13-15). At the Judgment Seat of Christ our work will be tested by the fire. Will we stand the test?

PRAYER: "Savior, help me today to build for eternity."

AUGUST 4

READING: 1 Corinthians 4

" ... for we are made a spectacle unto the world, and to angels, and to men." 1 Corinthians 4:9

The Christian life is meant to be quite different than any other kind of life. It is to be a Christ-controlled life, a life of self-denial, suffering and sacrifice. Paul says that for Christ we must be willing to endure several personal sacrifices. Personal HUMILIATION (vv. 9-10). The word, spectacle, is a vivid metaphor taken from the Greek amphitheatre. In the grand finale, defeated captives were dragged before the crowd like condemned animals, gaped at by heartless crowds. As a Christian expect nothing but jeers and indignities. Personal RENUNCIATION (vv. 11-13). The crucified life may expect perhaps physical and mental suffering. Millions of believers the world over are experiencing such. Personal ANNIHILATION (vv. 13). For Christ we might be regarded as the world's garbage, the scum of the universe.

PRAYER: "Lord Jesus, am I willing to be considered garbage for Jesus?"

AUGUST 5

READING: 1 Corinthians 5

"Your glorying is not good." 1 Corinthians 5:6

The church was planted in Corinth to change the city. Instead, the city was changing the church! This is not a pleasant devotional. Matters relative to how to deal with sin in the church are discussed. The purpose is to keep the church pure. Certain attitudes are necessary. HATEFULNESS in relation to sin (vv. 6-8). Leaven in the Bible is a picture of evil. Open sin must not be allowed in the church. HELPFULNESS in relation to the world (vv. 9-10). We aren't here to condemn nor condone the world. We are here to confront the world with a different kind of life. The idea is insulation, not isolation. HOLINESS in relation to the church (vv. 11-13). Strong words. But, keep in mind the purpose is not just to rid the church of sin, but to restore the sinning church member.

PRAYER: *"Lord, help me today to get the sin out of my life."*

AUGUST 6

READING: 1 Corinthians 6

" ... therefore glorify God in your body ..." 1 Corinthians 6:20

Every aspect of our person is affected by the salvation experience. Even the body. The body gets a lot of attention in our culture. But, in the wrong way. The believer's body is to be an instrument of righteousness. Our devotional verses today discuss this. The ELEVATION of the body (vv. 12-15a). Salvation elevates our body to a new level of liberty and sanctity. There are limits to our liberty. Not all things are helpful. The DESECRATION of the body (vv. 15b-18). Sexual sin is a desecration of our Savior. We must not join Christ to sexual immorality. Nor must we bring contamination to our own life. God's Word is to "Flee ..." The CONSECRATION of the body (vv. 19-20). Our body was bought and paid for when Jesus died at Calvary. The Holy Spirit dwells in our body. So, glorify God in your body!

PRAYER: *"Lord Jesus, I consecrate my body to You."*

AUGUST 7

READING: 1 Corinthians 7

> ## "And unto the married I command, yet not I, but the Lord ..."
> ## 1 Corinthians 7:10

This is a rather long chapter. Read part today and the rest tomorrow. The subject is marriage. God has some specific words to those who are married. We learn here how to be happily married. The MONOGAMY of Christian marriage (vv. 1-2). God's intention is for one man to be married to one woman. The relationship is to be one of sanctity and purity. The HARMONY of Christian marriage (v. 3-16). Oneness in marriage is to be physical (vv. 3-5), psychological (vv. 10-11) and spiritual (vv. 12-16). The PERMANENCY of Christian marriage (vv. 39-40). God's intention is that marriage is to be "only in the Lord." When you get married, ask yourself, Do I want to spend the rest of my life with this person?

PRAYER: *"Lord, I want to keep my part of the marriage commitment."*

AUGUST 8

READING: 1 Corinthians 7

> ## *"I say therefore to the unmarried and widows ..." 1 Corinthians 7:8*

Single? Felt left out yesterday? Not to worry. Today, God has something for you. We may have to pick through these verses, but there are some specific encouragements for singles. Here you will learn how to be happily unmarried. The NOBILITY of the single state (vv. 1,7-9,25-28). There is nothing wrong with being single. If it isn't God's will for you to marry, He can make you happy as a single. The MOBILITY of the single state (vv. 32-35). Actually, there are some advantages to it. You could miss out on some distress and distraction. The RESPONSIBILITY of the single state (vv. 36-40). If the Lord wants you to be married, He will send a mate to you. If not, He can use you as a single in a very special way.

PRAYER: *"Lord Jesus, You were single. I'm willing to be, if that is Your will."*

AUGUST 9

READING: 1 Corinthians 8

"Knowledge puffeth up, but charity edifieth." 1 Corinthians 8:1

At first glance Paul's words concerning meat offered to idols have nothing to do with us. But, closer examination will indicate he gives us some principles to follow in deciding about matters of right and wrong that aren't specifically addressed in the Bible. Three helpful principles to help us make these kinds of decisions are found here. The INTELLECTUAL Principle (vv. 1-4). Knowledge is mentioned 11 times in 1 Corinthians 8. Learn all you can about a questionable matter. Be sure your knowledge is controlled by humility and love. The SPIRITUAL Principle (vv. 5-8). When making decisions we must consider what is the reality of the matter. And could those who are immature spiritually be harmed? The SOCIAL Principle (vv. 9-13). Others are watching your life. Do not be "a stumbling block." Don't "wound" others.

PRAYER: "Lord, help me not to use my freedom to hurt others by what I do."

AUGUST 10

READING: 1 Corinthians 9

"But I have used none of these things ..." 1 Corinthians 9:15

The use of freedom tests one's Christian maturity. For 14 verses Paul defends his right to have support. Then, he renounces it! He moves from the principle of knowledge to the principle of love. He renounces his rights for the sake of the SAVIOR (vv. 12-15-18). He wants nothing he may do to make it hard for people to see Jesus. He renounces them for the sake of sinners (vv. 19-23). What a glorious paradox: we are free from all yet bound to all. This is not compromise but compassion. We must be willing to give up any right we have in order to lead others to Christ. He renounces them for the sake of HIMSELF (vv. 24-27). Like an athlete we must lay aside anything that will disqualify us from being victorious in the Christian life.

PRAYER: "Lord Jesus, I lay my rights aside for You and others."

AUGUST 11

READING: 1 Corinthians 10

"... do all to the glory of God." 1 Corinthians 10:31

The things we do or do not do have implications. Therefore, deciding matters of right and wrong must be guided by two great principles: everything we do must be for the glory of God and for the good of others (vv. 31-33). Thus, the things we do have SPIRITUAL implications (vv. 14-22). Our relation to the Lord is most vital. Our behavior will enhance our relationship to God or will damage it. We are to participate at the Divine table (vv. 16-18) and separate from the demonic table (vv. 19-22). The things we do have SOCIAL implications (vv. 23-30). We must take care that our actions not hinder others. "Don't cause others to stumble" is a recurring theme in the Bible. Our actions should help others.

PRAYER: "Lord, in everything I do today help me first to ask, will this bring glory to You and will it be good for others?"

AUGUST 12

READING: 1 Corinthians 11

"For I have received of the Lord that which also I delivered unto you ..." 1 Corinthians 11:23

In the midst of a chapter discussing abuses in worship is a beautiful passage about God's people gathering around the Lord's Supper Table. What a sweet time when God's people are together at the Table to which the Lord Jesus has invited us. Several spiritual exercises should be a part of this time. RECOLLECTION ("in remembrance ..."). The elements of the Supper call to mind again His broken body and His shed blood. EXPLANATION ("show the Lord's death ..."). The Lord's Supper is a great preacher, more eloquent than a Spurgeon, more earnest than a Graham. The bread and the cup become a silent sermon of all Jesus came to do. EXPECTATION ("Till He come."). We gather together in anticipation of the time when we will be "caught up together."

PRAYER: "Lord, may I faithfully gather with believers at Your Table."

AUGUST 13

READING: 1 Corinthians 14

"Now concerning spiritual gifts ..." 1 Corinthians 14:1

Christians have been given spiritual gifts (v. 11). Every believer has one or more (v. 7). The FOUNDATION of spiritual gifts (vv. 1-3). Believers are not to be carried away by the demonic (v. 2). There are many spirits at work in our world. Believers are to be controlled by the Divine (v. 3). True spirituality will always acknowledge that Jesus is Lord (v. 3). That is the most spiritual thing you can do. The VARIATION of spiritual gifts (vv. 4-6). This is a Divinely given variety that enables us to use our spiritual capacities ("gifts") in spiritual ministries ("administrations") with spiritual energies ("operations"). The MANIFESTATION of spiritual gifts (vv. 7-11). Spiritual gifts aren't toys to play with; they are tools to build with. They are not for enjoyment, but for employment. Whatever God has given you to serve Him, use it for His glory.

PRAYER: "Lord Jesus, thank You for giving me spiritual abilities to serve You."

AUGUST 14

READING: 1 Cotinthians 13

" ... but the greatest of these is charity (love)." 1 Corinthians 13:13

Love is the atmosphere where spiritual gifts are exercised. Love is the climate in which spiritual gifts are effective. This chapter is saturated with the importance of love in relationship to using spiritual gifts. The PRIORITY of love (vv. 1-3). Without love spiritual gifts are noise (v. 1). Clanging cymbals; blaring trumpets. Without love spiritual gifts are nothing (vv. 2-3). Add up all these spiritual activities—prophecy; faith; giving to the poor; martyrdom. No love? Push the calculator button. It equals zero. The PERSONALITY of love (vv. 4-7). This is how love will affect your life. A pefect picture of Jesus! Love will make you more like Jesus. The PERMANENCY of love (vv. 8-13). There are no signs of decay in love. It outlasts all the gifts (vv. 8-11). It outranks all the graces (vv. 12-13).

PRAYER: "Lord Jesus, may I make love my ambition."

AUGUST 15

READING: 1 Corinthians 14

"Let all things be done unto edifying." 1 Corinthians 14:26

D on't let the difficulties of this chapter cause you to miss the blessing for today. Paul is clearly minimizing tongues and magnifying prophecy. Prophecy today is the preaching of the Word of God. Some gifts in the church were intended for the early church until the canon of Scripture was completed. Now, the preaching of the Word is primary. Several things will take place when the Holy Spirit is in charge of our worship

SHARING ("come together," v. 23). This is referring to those times when God's people gather together for public worship. LEARNING ("understanding," v. 14). True worship engages the mind. God never bypasses our mind. GROWING ("edifying," v. 26). You ought to leave a worship service with spiritual food to help you grow. OBEYING ("decently and in order," v. 40). We must leave with the desire to obey God's Word.

PRAYER: "Lord, help me to allow You to build me up in my worship."

AUGUST 16

READING: 1 Corinthians 15:1-11

" ... I declare unto you the gospel ..." 1 Corinthians 15:1

W e must be very clear about what the Gospel really is. The word means, good news. The Gospel is God's good news about man's bad news. The bad news is that we are sinners and are going to die. God's good news is His provision for man's predicament. For the sin problem God provides the CRUCIFIXION of Christ (1 Corinthians 15:3-4a). On the cross Jesus paid for our sins. In the coffin He put away our sins. For the death problem God provides the RESURRECTION of Christ (1 Corinthians 15:3b-8). When Christ rose from the death He conquered death. In His post-resurrection appearances He demonstrated that to meet Him changes one's life forever. What good news!

PRAYER: "Lord Jesus, thank You for dying on the cross for me and for being alive forever to change my life and give me hope in death."

AUGUST 17

READING: 1 Corinthians 15:12-58

"But thanks be to God, which giveth us the victory through our Lord Jesus Christ." 1 Corinthians 15:57

Because Jesus rose from the dead so shall we! This glorious resurrection chapter fills our hearts with great joy, peace and anticipation. There is indeed victory in Jesus. Our victory involves PERSONAL REALITY (1 Corinthians 1:50-53). How wonderful to know that we will experience the change because of our relationship with the living Christ. Living and dead believers will be changed. Our victory involves POWERFUL REALIZATION (1 Corinthians 15:54-57). Death is pictured here as a fearful monster with a poisonous sting. Jesus took the sting out of death. Our victory involves PRACTICAL RESULTS (1 Corinthians 15:58). When we claim Christ's victory in our daily life we will be "stedfast and unmoveable ..." Because the tomb is empty our labor is not empty! Victory in Jesus!

PRAYER: "Lord Jesus, today may I claim the victory You have given me."

AUGUST 18

READING: 1 Corinthians 16

"Now concerning the collection ..." 1 Corinthians 16:1

We move from the resurrection to the collection. The Christian faith is not only deeply spiritual, but supremely practical. We belong to two worlds: in the heavenly and in the here and now. So, collections must be taken for God's work. Our giving must be PUNCTUAL ("Upon the first day of the week ..."). When we gather in the Lord's House we must bring something to give the Lord. It must be PERSONAL (" ... let every one of you ..."). God wants us all to participate in giving to the work of the Lord. It must be PROPORTIONAL (" ... as God hath prospered him ..."). A percentage seems to be indicated. A good starting place is the tithe (10%). Not as a law, but an act of love. It must be PRACTICAL (" ... no gatherings when I come"). When we give the work of the Lord is funded and we are blessed.

PRAYER: "Thank You, Lord Jesus, for the joy of giving."

AUGUST 19

READING: 2 Corinthians 1

" ... the God of all comfort ..." 2 Corinthians 1:4

Life has its troubles. We daily need relief. We have a God who can give us comfort. The EXISTENCE of it (2 Corinthians 1:3-4). Comfort is available because of who God is. He is "the Father of mercies, and the God of all comfort" (v. 3). It is also available because of what God does. He comforts us. The moment trouble comes God's heart goes out to you. The EXPERIENCE of it (vv. 4b, 6). God's comfort is something we experience through the Scriptures (Romans 15:4) and the Holy Spirit (John 14:18). We also have the privilege of passing God's comfort on to others who are having troubles. God wants you to be a channel for His comfort. The EXTRAVAGANCE of it (vv. 5,7). God's comfort "abounds". It will overflow in our life like a river overflowing its banks.

PRAYER: "Thank You today, Heavenly Father, for Your comfort."

AUGUST 20

READING: 2 Corinthians 2

"Now thanks be unto God which always causeth us to triumph in Christ ..." 2 Corinthians 2:14

We can experience victory in our daily life. Using the background of a victorious Roman triumphal march Paul pictures our victory in Christ. The SAVIOR SECURES it (v. 14a). We are following in the train of the Captain of our Salvation. On the cross He "spoiled" and "showed" the enemy (Colossians 2:15). The SAINT SHARES in it (vv. 14b). "Always" indicates we can experience continal, perpetual victory over the forces of satan and sin. The SAVIOR SPREADS it (vv. 15-16). Our life can be a precious aroma to the Father, a pleasant aroma to the saved, and a perilous aroma to the lost. There should be a fragrance to our life like that of Mary's perfume filling the room (John 12:3).

PRAYER: "Help me today to be a pleasant fragrance to those who come into contact with me."

AUGUST 21

READING 2 Corinthians 3

> *"We ... are changed into the same image from glory to glory ..."*
> *2 Corinthians 3:18*

Salvation restores to us the glory lost by the fall (Romans 3:23). Salvation is glorious in its transforming power. This transforming glory begins in SALVATION (vv. 12-17). When we turn to the Lord there is a change at the deepest level of our being. The veil is lifted from our heart and glory is restored in our hearts. This transforming glory continues in SANCTIFICATION (v. 18). Sanctification is progressive growth in righteousness. It is the process whereby God gets the glory within you to the outside of your life. One of the ways God does this is by our study of the Word of God. The child of God looks into the Word of God, sees the Son of God and is changed into the image of God by the Spirit of God unto the glory of God.

PRAYER: *"Lord, may I let You get the glory into my daily life today."*

AUGUST 22

READING: 2 Corinthians 4

> *" ... for the things which are seen are temporal ..." 2 Corinthians 4:18*

We sometimes make the mistake of looking at life only from the temporary point of view. We should live our life with eternity in view. This is especially true when it comes to our troubles. Paul says our "afflictions" are "light." They certainly don't seem light, do they? We must link our troubles with two spiritual realities. GLORY (v. 17). They "work for us." God is putting our troubles to work for us. This is not to belittle what you are going through. Rather, it is saying that God uses them to bring more glory into your life. ETERNITY (v. 18). Keep in mind the big picture. The real world is the eternal, unseen world. Keep this thought before you today: One hundred years from now you will be in eternity. Live your life looking at things unseen.

PRAYER: *"Lord Jesus, help me to look unto You today, for You are my eternal Savior."*

AUGUST 23

READING: 2 Corinthians 5

" ... if any man be in Christ, he is a new creature ..." 2 Corinthians 5:17

People talk about having a makeover. The desire is to make one's self look better than ever before. For the Christian this is what sanctification is all about. God is making a brand new you. You have a brand new POSITION ("in Christ"). Before salvation we were located spiritually "in Adam." (1 Corinthians 15:22). Now, we are "in Christ," in a new position spiritually. You have a brand new PERSONALITY ("new creation"). Salvation is not a renovation or reformation. It is a regeneration. Just like in God's work of creation (Genesis 1:1), salvation makes something out of nothing! When God created the physical world it cost Him some of His soil. When He creates a new person it takes the blood of His Son. You have a brand new POTENTIAL ("old things ... new"). The old has gone; the new has come.

PRAYER: "Lord, thanks for my makeover."

AUGUST 24

READING: 2 Corinthians 6

"Wherefore come out ..." 2 Corinthians 6:17

Bible separation is much neglected by Christians. But, the Bible is clear that separation is a part of sanctification. Sanctification means positively to come to Christ to become like Him. Negatively it is to come out from the world. This isn't to make your life miserable, but to make it joyful. God attaches a wonderful promise to this call for separation. There is the promise of the Father's FAVOR ("I will receive you ..." v. 17). At salvation God becomes our Father. We share His life as a member of His family. To be separated from the world means we enter into His love. We do not want anything to displease Him nor to cause us to lose the enjoyment of His love. There is the promise of the Father's FELLOWSHIP ("And will be a Father unto you ..." v. 18). To walk in fellowship with the Father is glorious separation.

PRAYER: "Father, today I choose You over the world."

AUGUST 25

READING: 2 Corinthians 7

"... perfecting holiness in the fear of God." 2 Corinthians 7:1

Yesterday the negative side of sanctification, separation, was set before us. Today, there is a positive side in addition to the negative side. Postively, to be separated is to be consecrated to God. The Bible word is "holiness." Look at the PATTERN of holiness. Holiness involves the negative (" ... let us cleanse ourselves ..."). But, holiness is incomplete unless we seek to be consecrated unto the image of Christ. Look at the PROMISE of holiness. Mention is made of the promises of God. God promises that one day we will be like Christ. We should aspire to realize that promise in our daily life. Look at the PROCESS of holiness ("perfecting holiness ..."). This process is to be followed (Hebrews 12:14). Holiness is to spiritual life what health is to physical life. To be a balanced, healthy, whole person is to be like Jesus.

PRAYER: "Lord Jesus, may I today pursue holiness."

AUGUST 26

READING: 2 Corinthians 8

"... but first gave their own selves to the Lord ..." 2 Corinthians 8:5

To learn to be a giver is one of the greatest lessons to be learned in the Christian life. By nature most of us are takers. To become a giver is a work of God's grace in our life. These verses should guide our church giving. The truth that true giving is grace giving, is highlighted in 2 Corinthians 8. The principle of LIBERALITY in giving (vv. 1-5). Let's don't give until it hurts; let's give until it feels good! The true source of all generosity is a surrendered life. The principle of SINCERITY in giving (vv. 6-9). Grace giving is born of pure motives. Christ is our great example of sincerity in that He gave Himself. The principle of EQUALITY in giving (vv. 10-15). " ... by an equality ..." Verse 14 indicates that there is a fairness in grace giving. We must all do our part.

PRAYER: "Help me to learn to be a grace giver."

AUGUST 27

READING: 2 Corinthians 9

" ... for God loveth a cheerful giver." 2 Corinthians 9:7

Again today we read about the matter of giving. God is interested in what you give; He is more interested in how you give. We should give with several attitudes. READINESS (vv. 1-5). We must be ready to give as we have committed. Perhaps you have committed yourself to give to your church. Be ready to do it. BOUNTIFULNESS (vv. 6, 8-11). Like the laws of sowing and reaping, giving involves God's abundant blessings upon us. This doesn't mean you will be rich if you give. It means you will have your needs met and have spiritual blessings in your life. CHEERFULNESS (v. 7). The word, "cheerful," literally means hilarious. God doesn't want sad givers, mad givers, but glad givers. THANKFULNESS (vv. 12-15). Giving is a part of worship. When we get and when we give we should be thankful.

PRAYER: "Lord, today I will become a happy giver."

AUGUST 28

READING: 2 Corinthians 10

"But he that glorieth, let him glory in the Lord." 2 Corinthians 10:17

In this chapter Paul is responding to those who are attacking him. Thankfully, for us, there is provided a series of pictures illustrating what it means to live the Christian life. I'm a SOLDIER (vv. 1-6)! We are in a battle against spiritual strongholds. God has provided us with the spiritual weapons of His Word and prayer. I'm a BUILDER (v. 7-11)! Though some were taunting him about his personal appearance, he didn't let this sway him. Builders don't have to be pretty. They have to be edifiers, building up God's people. I'm a PIONEER (vv. 12-18)! We look to new frontiers to conquer for Christ (v. 16). There is always new territory to conquer for Christ. Whether another land, or some pocket of unbelief where we are.

PRAYER: "Lord, help me today to be more interested in Your work that in what others think of me."

AUGUST 29

READING: 2 Corinthians 11

> *" ... that I may present you as a chaste virgin to Christ."*
> *2 Corinthians 11:2*

The church is compared to many things: an army; a family; a building; a body. Here, the church is compared to a bride. Several concerns emerge about the church as the bride of Christ. The PURITY of the Bride (v. 2). Saved people have been "espoused," or engaged to Christ. God wants us to be pure. What a great incentive to live a clean life. When tempted to stain our body or spirit, we must remember, "I'm spoken for." The SIMPLICITY of the Bride (v. 3). Simplicity here means single-hearted faith in Christ. Don't let Satan deceive you as he did Eve and Adam in the garden. The FIDELITY of the Bride (v. 4). Stay true to the Savior, who saves us; the Holy Spirit who sanctifies us; the Gospel, that satisfies us!

PRAYER: "Lord, today may I be a pure bride, awaiting that great wedding in the sky."

AUGUST 30

READING: 2 Corinthians 12

> *"My grace is sufficient for thee ..." 2 Corinthians 12:9*

We really don't know what Paul's thorn in the flesh was. Whatever it was, it was like a stake driven into his flesh. But, as it should us, his problem drove him to God's promises. Paul's REQUEST (v. 8). As do we so often, Paul prayed to escape the problem. God doesn't always answer our prayers with, yes. Sometimes He says, no. Or, wait. Which leads us today to God's RESPONSE (vv. 9-10). God promises sufficient grace. What a promise! We are not told God's grace will be sufficient sometime in the future. God says, "My grace IS …" Right now. Bring the little teacup of your trouble to the vast ocean of God's grace. Whatever you are facing today God's grace is adequate and it is available.

PRAYER: "Lord, I am glad whatever may come my way, it will not take You by surprise and You have Your grace ready to help me."

AUGUST 31

READING: 2 Corinthians 13

"Examine yourselves, whether ye be in the faith ..." 2 Corinthians 13:5

It is a good thing to periodically check up on our life. A spiritual inventory is needed from time to time. Today let's have three questions to guide our personal examination. Is there PURITY in my life (vv. 1-4)? Sins of the disposition and flesh can break out. The solution is found in Christ's death at the cross and His resurrection power in our life. Is there REALITY in my life (vv. 5-8)? Is it really true that I am in the faith? The only adequate measure is the Word of God. Have I repented of my sin and am I trusting Christ as my personal Savior? Is there MATURITY in my life (vv. 9-14)? The idea is expressed in "perfection" (v. 9) and in "Be perfect" (v. 11). Am I moving forward in my growth in Christlikeness?

PRAYER: "Lord, I fall short, but I trust in You."

September

KINGS ON PARADE.

*This month we will witness
a parade of Old Testament
Kings, and observe a couple
of prophets speaking truth to
power. Saul. David. Solomon.
Rehoboam. And more. Elijah.
Elisha. Let's learn vital truths
from them.*

SEPTEMBER 1

READING: 1 Samuel 31

" ... the Philistines came to strip the slain ..." 1 Samuel 31:8

Saul is a tragic enigma in the Bible. There was greatness in the man. But, also weakness. Things started off positively (See 1 Samuel 9-11). He was humble and spiritual. But his persistent bitterness toward David leads to a downward spiral into degradation and ruin. His life ends in tragedy. SENTENCED (1 Samuel 28:1ff). Heaven's door was barred to him, so he knocked on the door of hell. SLAIN (1 Samuel 31:3ff). He knows what is ahead, so he falls on his own sword. STRIPPED (1 Samuel 31:8ff). If you choose sin, one day in the future the devil will come and strip you of everything you value in your life. Saul's biggest problem was he couldn't bow the knee to David, God's chosen king. We must not play the fool and refuse to bow the knee to King Jesus.

PRAYER: "Lord, may I not be a Saul."

SEPTEMBER 2

READING: 1 Samuel 16

" ... the Spirit of the Lord came upon David from that day forward." 1 Samuel 16:13

David is mentioned 600 times in the Old Testament; 60 times in the New Testament. God says David is "a man after (His) own heart" (1 Samuel 13:14). God had a plan for David's life, as He does for yours. APPOINTED To God's PLAN (vv. 1-11). The focus is not David, but God. God knows what He is doing and the person He wants to do His work. ANOINTED By God's PROPHET (vv. 12-13). Samuel anoints David's head with oil. Three offices were anointed: the prophet; the priest; the king. When God gives you a job He will give you His power to do it. ASSOCIATED With God's PEOPLE (vv. 14-23). He is to be the leader of God's people. But, something else is here. David, meet Saul. Do you have a Saul?

PRAYER: "Lord, I need Your anointing for what is ahead."

SEPTEMBER 3

READING: **1 Samuel 17**

" *... for the battle is the Lord's ...*" *1 Samuel 17:47*

David vs. Goliath is well known in Bible stories. You may remember it from children's Sunday School. We learn how to overcome seemingly insurmountable odds and win the victory over giant problems. Goliath's CHALLENGE (vv. 1-11). Goliath is big (vv. 4-7) and blasphemous (vv. 8-11). What is your giant? Does it taunt you? David's CONFESSION (vv. 12-37). David had been preparing for this big battle with smaller ones previously. Private battles prepare us for public ones. Little battles prepare us for big battles. God's CONQUEST (vv. 38-58). You have God's provision. Don't fight spiritual battles with untested armor. "The battle is the Lord's." Never forget this. Two or three loops of David's sling and the stone is hurled. Splat! Smash! Victory! Facing giants can be scary. Trust God for your victory. We don't fight for victory, but from victory!

PRAYER: "Lord, today I face my giants in Your victory."

SEPTEMBER 4

READING: **1 Samuel 20**

"The Lord be between me and thee ..." 1 Samuel 20:42

David is on the run. Jealous, bitter Saul sends him running. He is now a fugitive. Just when he needs him, Jonathan, his true friend, steps into the picture. Samuel Johnson said, "A real friend is one who will tell you your faults and failures in prosperity and will assist you with his hand and heart in adversity." David's APPEAL (vv. 1-23). Sometimes people are against us for reasons unknown to us. Have you ever raised questions like David's (v. 1)? David's ABSENCE (vv. 24-34). Everyone is at Saul's table but David. There is no doubt. Saul intends to kill David. David's AGREEMENT (vv. 35-42). Witness the touching scene between David and his friend, Jonathan. When your heart is broken, a friend understands and weeps with you. Do you have a friend like Jonathan? You have a friend in Jesus!

PRAYER: "Lord, what a friend I have in Jesus!"

SEPTEMBER 5

READING: 1 Samuel 23

> " *... and strengthened his hand in God."* 1 Samuel 23:16

Davi d heads to caves to escape murderous Saul. Caves come in the life of all. David learns valuable lessons in caves, as shall we. Several encouragments are available for the cave experiences. The encouragement of PRAYER (vv. 1-15). In verse 2 and again in verse 4 David prays. In prayer we seek God's wisdom and guidance. There is something better than the Urim and Thummim to guide us. The Word of God. The encouragement of PEOPLE (vv. 16-18). Who shows up in these cave days? Jonathan! He risks his life to encourage his friend and "strengthen his hand in God." He puts David's hand in God's hand. That's a good friend. The encouragement of PROVIDENCE (vv. 19-29). David seems to be trapped by Saul. But, an unexpected attack and Saul is diverted. God works in unusual ways to providentially deliver us.

PRAYER: "Lord, I place my hand in Yours today."

SEPTEMBER 6

READING: 1 Samuel 24

> " *... I will not put forth mine hand against my Lord ..."* 1 Samuel 24:10

Do you have an enemy? David did. Saul! David has done nothing to Saul, but he was Saul's enemy. David teaches us how to deal with an enemy. His OPPORTUNITY (vv. 1-4). David had the opportunity to harm Saul. What do you do when you can retaliate against an enemy? David takes the position of non-retaliation (Matthew 5:43-44). His HUMILITY (vv. 5-11). Saul was his enemy; and his king. David is humble enough to submit to authority. If we have trouble with authority, we are in rebellion against God (Judges 21:25). His SINCERITY (vv. 12-22). David calls on God to witness to his sincerity. If you want to see how mature you are as a Christian, see what you do when your enemy is in your control. Judgment is God's prerogative (Romans 12:17-21).

PRAYER: "Lord, today I turn my enemy over to You."

SEPTEMBER 7

READING: 1 Samuel 25

> ### *"Blessed be the Lord God of Israel, which sent thee this day to meet me ..." 1 Samuel 25:32*

Davel was a man "after God's own heart," but that doesn't mean he always did the right thing. His encounter with Nabal is a dangerous episode in his life. The REQUEST Nabal DENIES (vv. 1-13). Nabal was a rich man, but also a thick-headed clod! David's simple request is met with a smart-mouthed response. David is a red-head with a temper. Anger is a learned reaction to frustration. He loses all sense of who he is and where he is headed. The RAID Abigail DEFLECTS (vv. 14-35). Thank God for Abigail's wisdom. She speaks to David with spiritual insight. Abigail is God's stop sign. Thank God for the "Abigails" who keep us from evil. The RETRIBUTION God DELIVERS (vv. 36-44). God will take care of your Nabals.

PRAYER: "Lord, may I not let anger cause me to be stupid."

SEPTEMBER 8

READING: 1 Samuel 28

> ### *" ... when Saul inquired of the Lord, the Lord answered him not ..." 1 Samuel 28:6*

God won't answer Saul's prayer. When separated from God, people seek elsewhere for guidance. Saul's DESPERATION (vv. 3-6). Though Saul had banned witches, in his desperation he seeks one himself. Saul's DECEPTION (vv. 7-19). Getting no word from heaven, Saul knocks on the door of hell. We don't know exactly how to interpret this scene. One thing is sure— Saul has been drifting in the waters of destruction; he is now in the rapids. Saul's DEJECTION (vv. 20-25). Saul is now terminal. Not one sign of remorse nor desire to be forgiven by God. Saul leaves the witch's house a walking dead man. He had only two choices: to acknowledge David as king or to turn to the devil. He chose the latter and it brought death. The choice is the same today: Jesus or Satan; life or death.

PRAYER: "Lord Jesus, today I choose You and life."

SEPTEMBER 9

READING: 1 Samuel 30

> *"... but David encouraged himself in the Lord his God." 1 Samuel 30:6*

Davd was on the verge of becoming a king and almost blew it. But, God graciously intervenes in a series of events. David is kicked out of enemy land. Things look bad. Now he looks up. The CHANGE (vv. 6-8). In his time of need he seeks the Lord. "Encouraged" means he found the Lord's strength. When there is nothing in circumstances nor from our friends to encourage us, there is encouragement in the Lord. The CHASE (vv. 9-15). He pursues with 400 men while 200 stayed behind and watched the supplies. God always works with two groups: those who go; those who stay. Both are important to the work of the Lord. The CONQUEST (vv. 16-20). David recovered all that had been lost. What we lost by sin Jesus recovered by the cross and the empty tomb!

PRAYER: "Lord, I am thankful for the encouragment of Your victory."

SEPTEMBER 10

READING: 2 Samuel 1

> *"And David lamented with this lamentation ..." 2 Samuel 1:17*

1 Samuel 31 and 2 Samuel 1 are like scenes of a movie, moving back and forth between Saul and David. 3 words flash on the screen: DEATH (1 Samuel 31:2-6); DISGRACE (1 Samuel 31:7-13); DIRGE (2 Samuel 1)! The death is Saul's; the dirge is David's. The SAD REPORT (vv. 1-16). When David gets the report of Saul and his beloved friend, Jonathan, the words stab his heart. Have you lost a loved one or friend recently? Sadness is normal and to be expected. The SOLEMN RESPECT (vv. 17-27). Out of his sadness David composes a funeral dirge to honor Saul and Jonathan. Not one unkind word about Saul. He doesn't say, "The maniac is dead. Let me tell you what a scoundrel he was." No. "Love suffers long and is kind."

PRAYER: "Lord, may I learn to handle death with grace and respect."

SEPTEMBER 11

READING: 2 Samuel 2-4

> "*... but David waxed stronger and stronger, and the house of Saul waxed weaker and weaker.*" 2 Samuel 3:1

David's march to the throne of Israel was not easy, and 2 Samuel 2-4 are chapters of blood and death. There are three murders. The murder of a BROTHER (2 Samuel 2). Abner was commander of Saul's army. He had led the hunt for David. He sets up a rival kingdom to David's. When the bloody chapter is over, Ashael is dead. The murder of a COMMANDER (2 Samuel 3). Joab, David's commander, steps on the stage. When this chapter is over, Abner is dead. The murder of a USURPER (2 Samuel 4). Ishbosheth who would usurp David's throne is murdered in this chapter. Why such a bloody devotion today? The Bible is a book about real life. God can work in spite of human sin and failure.

PRAYER: "*Lord, I look at the violence and bloodshed in our world. Help me to also look up to You.*"

SEPTEMBER 12

READING: 2 Samuel 25

> "*... when thou hearest the sound of a going in the tops of the mulberry trees ... bestir thyself ...*" 2 Samuel 5:24

David is king. For years he was on the run, fearing for his life. Now, the nation consolidates under him. The CROWNING of David (vv. 1-5). David is a picture of the Lord Jesus, our Shepherd-King. We should bow to the Lord Jesus as our king (Philippians 2:10-11); one day all shall (Romans 14:11). The CITY of David (vv. 6-16). David needs a capital city. He chooses Jerusalem. How David took Jerusalem is a fascinating read. David is aware he is king because of the Lord. Are you aware your success is of the Lord? The CONQUEST of David (vv. 17-25). There are battles for David to fight. The wind blowing in the balsam trees reminds us that we must not move until He moves!

PRAYER: "*Lord, let me hear the rustling of the leaves today.*"

SEPTEMBER 13

READING: 2 Samuel 6

"So David ... brought up the ark ... with gladness." 2 Samuel 6

King David realizes the worship of God must be re-instituted to its rightful place. The ark, that wooden chest, covered with the golden mercy seat, must be brought up to Jerusalem. Vital worship lessons are learned. Worship DESECRATED (vv. 1-11). David is trying to worship God man's way, not God's way. There are a lot of new carts in our churches today. God always judges desecration in worship. Worship DESCRIBED (vv. 12-15,17-19). David must have searched his Bible. When God's people worship correctly God shows up in the midst of the people. Worship DESPISED (vv. 16, 20-23). David's wife, Michal despises what she sees. There is no indecency here. David just dresses himself in a simple garment and worships along with the people. Dignity in worship is desirable. But, some poor saints mistake deadness for dignity.

PRAYER: "Lord may my worship be dignified, but not petrified."

SEPTEMBER 14

READING: 2 Samuel 7

" ... do as thou hast said. And let thy name be magnified forever ..." 2 Samuel 7:25-26

David dreams big dreams. He wants to build a place where God will be worshiped. This chapter is crucial to understanding the New Testament and God's eternal plan. David's PROPOSAL (vv. 1-3). What a noble thing to want to do something for God. Nathan the prophet likes David's proposal. David wants to be a giver instead of a receiver. David's PROMISE (vv. 4-17). God declines David's sincere plan. God will allow a Temple to be built. But, David's son, Solomon, will build it. Ultimately, the Lord Jesus will fulfill this promise (Luke 1:28-33). David's PRAYER (vv. 18-29). Not one note of bitterness is found in David's prayer. Whatever God's plan for us may be, we should let is cause us to praise and pray.

PRAYER: "Lord, today I make big plans. I'm willing to surrender them to Your better plans."

SEPTEMBER 15

READING: 2 Samuel 9

"What is thy servant, that thou shouldest look upon such a dead dog as I am?" 2 Samuel 9:8

Just the mention of Mephibosheth makes us think of kindness, generosity, and grace. What David does for Mephibosheth pictures God's grace to us. God's grace SEEKS us (vv. 1-2). David wants to show Saul's house "kindness for Jonathan's sake"(v. 1). Though crippled by a fall like Mephibosheth, God wants to save us for Jesus' sake. God's grace SAVES us (vv. 6-8). We can only imagine how it must have been when Mephibosheth came into the King's presence. Grace restores all that our father, Adam, lost and seats us at the table of God's blessings. God's grace SATISFIES us (vv. 9-13). God satisfies us with provision (v. 9-11a) and position (vv. 11b-13). God's grace takes us from the place of emptiness to the place of fullness. Amazing Grace, indeed!

PRAYER: *"O God, thank You for Your grace for Jesus' sake."*

SEPTEMBER 16

READING: 2 Samuel 12

"Thou art the man." 2 Samuel 12:7

Think of David and two names come to mind: Goliath and Bathsheba. His greatest victory and his greatest defeat. David never thought people would read about it in their daily devotions. Aren't we glad God doesn't do our sins that way? Adultery led to murder and then to cover-up. For nine months David played the hypocrite. But, God uses his friend, Nathan the prophet, to expose his sin. CONFRONTATION (vv. 1-12). "Thou art the man," said Nathan. Those words hit David like a sledge hammer. David is seeing the truth of Proverbs 28:13 lived out in his own life. CONFESSION (vv. 13). David comes clean about his sin, saying, "I have sinned." We have just a few ways to sin; God has infinite ways to forgive. COMPLICATION (vv. 12:14-31). God forgave David, but didn't spare him the consequences.

PRAYER: *"Lord, thank You for grace to be forgiven and grace also to bear the consequences of my sin."*

SEPTEMBER 17

READING: 2 Samuel 18

"O Absalom, my son, my son." 2 Samuel 18:33

The account of Absalom, David's son, is one of the saddest episodes in the Bible. A son rebelling against his father. Absalom did to his own father, a good man, what David never did to Saul, a bad man. He stole his kingdom. Now we read the closing chapter. A SOLEMN COMMAND (vv. 1-8). David devises a strategy to defeat Absalom. But, his word is "deal gently … with the young man." A SAD CONQUEST (vv. 9-18). Caught in the thick branches of a large oak tree, he dies a violent death. A SERIOUS COMMUNIQUE (vv. 19-33). Picture David waiting at the gates. He hears the horrifying words that Absalom is dead. "O my son …" are some of the saddest, most heart wrenching words ever spoken. They erupt from David's grief-stricken heart. Children may break the hearts of their parents.

PRAYER: *"Father, today I pray for my children."*

SEPTEMBER 18

READING: 2 Samuel 19

" … why speak ye not a word of bringing the king back?"
2 Samuel 19:10

The attitudes some had about bringing David back to his kingdom illustrate for us how some view the return of the Lord Jesus. Shimei: Those who are HATEFUL (vv. 16-23). Shimei certainly was no friend of David (See 16:5-14). But, he wants to get on the victory train. Mephibosheth: Those who are FAITHFUL (vv. 24-30). He wanted to be like David until he returned. Do we want to be like Christ? May we be at His feet when He returns. Barzillai: Those who are FEARFUL (vv. 31-40). He had stood with David in tough times. But, he gives to another his reward. Chimham got it, part of which was some land near Bethlehem. Jesus came there! Let us be careful we don't let someone else get the reward for serving Jesus that could have been ours (Revelation 3:11).

PRAYER: *"Lord, I say today, 'Even so, come, Lord Jesus'."*

SEPTEMBER 19

READING: 2 Samuel 24

"... I have sinned greatly ..." 2 Samuel 24:10

As an old man David still has his problems. Old age doesn't make life easier; very often it gets harder. Though David is faithful to the end, he is also fallible. Temptation is tailor-made for our age category. SIN (vv. 1-9). The census itself was not wrong. But, evidently the pride which caused David to do it is the problem. Too often we are stubborn and want to have our own way. SUFFERING (vv. 10-17). What David thought would bring him pleasure brought him pain. And it caused others to suffer. When we sin we cause others to suffer. SACRIFICE (vv. 18-25). Only sacrifice could stop the suffering David's sin caused. God's forgiveness is available at all of life's stages. We never get too old to sin. The eternal God never gets too old to forgive!

PRAYER: "Lord, today may I realize I can sin regardless of my age."

SEPTEMBER 20

READING: 1 Kings 2

"And keep the charge of the Lord thy God ..." 1 Kings 2:3

The final days of David have come. Death is drawing near. Often preparing to die is more difficult than death itself. He has final arrangements to make. David props himself up on thin hands, trembling with age. He must choose his successor. Adonijah grabs the throne for himself. But, David chooses Solomon. The CHOICE (1 Kings 1:29-53). Evidently David had not established a clear transition plan. As we approach death we should take care that proper arrangements are made and understandings are achieved. The CHARGE (2:1-11). Note that David instructs Solomon concerning spiritual matters before he deals with political ones. What words of counsel would you give your children before you die? David's speech to Solomon rises on the tide of inspiration. Then, he falls on his knees and prays. What a legacy to leave a son.

PRAYER: "Father, I would be wise in my final words."

SEPTEMBER 21

READING: 1 Kings 11

"... his heart was not perfect with the Lord his God ..." 1 Kings 11:4

Solomon was the great son of a greater father. He may have written three Old Testament books (Song of Solomon; Proverbs; Ecclesiastes). When he was young he was wise. When he grew old he became a fool. He may be the most disappointing character in Israel's history. His MISTAKES (11:1, 4). He "loved many strange women ..." (v. 1). Perhaps as political arrangements, he married the daughters of pagan kings. His immorality led to idolatry (v. 4). These strange wives brought their gods with them. And his wives "turned away his heart" (v. 3). Soon his mistakes led to his MISERY (11:41-43). Solomon wrote a book about his last years. It isn't a happy book. Ecclesiastes tells of his search for happiness. Hopefully he returned to God at last (Ecclesiastes 12:1).

PRAYER: "Heavenly Father, as I get older, may I not turn to other gods that cannot satisfy."

SEPTEMBER 22

READING: 1 Kings 12

"Wherefore the king hearkened not unto the people ..." 1 Kings 12:15

Solomon became an old fool. Rehoboam was a young one. His foolish decision at the beginning of his reign defines his life. We learn a lot about a leader by how he responds to the difficult situations that confront him. The CRISIS (vv. 1-5). The people want him to be lighter on them than his father had been. Solomon had made life hard on them. It was a reasonable request. Rehoboam asks for time. Did he pray? No evidence he did. Did he consult a prophet? There is no mention. Where you go during a time of crisis is very revealing. The COUNSEL (vv. 6-15). The older men give him good advice. Rehoboam evidently has his mind made up already. He turns to the younger men. Their counsel is harsh, hasty and immature. Hot-headed leadership does much harm.

PRAYER: "Lord, may I always be willing to heed good, mature counsel."

SEPTEMBER 23

READING: 1 Kings 17

" ... hide thyself ..." 1 Kings 17:3

Elijah is one of the best-known Old Testament characters. Elijah reminds us that God always has His witness in apostate times. Elijah steps suddenly upon the Bible stage. "As the Lord God of Israel liveth ... not be dew nor rain ..." Elijah proved God was alive privately. At a brook Elijah proved God is alive in the COMMONPLACE experiences of life (vv. 2-7). Life must have been pretty boring by a brook. Your life seem rather commonplace? Ah, but God sends ravens to feed His prophet. Where God leads He feeds; where He guides He provides. By a barrel he proved He is alive in the CRISIS experiences of life (vv. 8-16). God will meet your need in those difficult times. With a boy he found God is alive in the CALAMITY experiences of life (vv. 17-23). Got a wayward child? Give him/her to God.

PRAYER: *"Lord Jesus, thank You for being real in my life."*

SEPTEMBER 24

READING: 1 Kings 18

" ... shew thyself ..." 1 Kings 18:1

The key to Elijah's life privately is "hide thyself." The key to his public ministry is "show thyself." We can prove God is alive publicly after we have proved Him alive in the privacy of our own experience. God is alive as Elijah CONFRONTS evil (vv. 19-40). The rumble on Mt. Carmel is dramatic beyond description. Elijah says, let's have a contest and see whose God is alive. When Elijah rebuilds the altar (v. 30) the sky crackles and flames from heaven's stockpiles embrace the altar. The rocks of Carmel ring as if a silver bells, "The Lord is God ..." (v. 39). God is alive as Elijah CLAIMS rain (vv. 41-46). Elijah prayed with such fervor that his uplifted hand stamped itself upon the sky. Hear him running down the mountain singing, "I've seen fire and I've seen rain!" God is alive.

PRAYER: *"Lord, thank You that You can send fire or rain, whichever is needed."*

SEPTEMBER 25

READING: 1 **Kings** 19

"It is enough; now, O Lord, take away my life ..." 1 Kings 19:4

Is this the same man who stood down Baal's prophets on Mt. Carmel? Elijah has moved from great courage to great despair. Very often times of great elation are followed by great dejection. Let's follow Elijah. Under a TREE: DEPRESSION (vv. 1-8). Elijah loses his nerve in the face of wicked Jezebel. He is tired, hungry and burned out. Note how tenderly God deals with his prophet. Sometimes we need some good food and rest. In a CAVE: REVELATION (vv. 9-18). God often speaks to us in a "still small voice." (v. 12). We should be encouraged to know God has His 7,000 faithful. On the ROAD: CONTINUATION (vv. 19-21). With renewed strength God sends Elijah to anoint a prophet and a king. Elijah prayed to die. God gave him strength to live and to serve another day.

PRAYER: "Dear God, today, give me strength."

SEPTEMBER 26

READING: 1 **Kings** 21

"Hast thou found me, O mine enemy?" 1 Kings 21:20

R. G. Lee made the account of Ahab and Elijah famous with his sermon, "Pay Day Someday." Ahab's selfish desire to have Naboth's vineyard and his wicked wife's plan to get it set the stage. Jezebel's DETERMINATION (vv. 5-11). She goads her husband king into a shameful death. The support of a good wife makes average men great. The degeneracy of womanhood leads to the decay of manhood. Naboth's DEATH (vv. 12-16). Ahab gets his vineyard with the blood of Naboth. A wife is bereft of her husband. Children lose a father. What does Ahab care? He heads to his treacherously obtained vineyard. Elijah's DECLARATION (vv. 17-23). Where is God? Jezebel said to Ahab, Arise, get your vineyard. God said to Elijah, Arise, go meet Ahab (v. 18). God sends a judgment message to Ahab. It was truly payday someday.

PRAYER: "Oh Lord, I thank You that You do judge wrongdoing."

SEPTEMBER 27

READING: 2 Kings 4

> *" ... I perceive that this is an holy man of God ..." 2 Kings 4:9*

Elijah goes to heaven. Enter Elisha. God brings his prophets on the scene at crucial times in history. His ministry to the Shunamite woman is a blessing. Her CHAMBER (vv. 8-10). She is called a "great woman." The Bible is careful of superlatives. There are reasons for her greatness. She show spiritual perception (vv. 8-9) and makes practical preparation (v. 10). Her CHILD (vv. 11-21). In keeping with Elisha's word God gives her a little boy! But, heartache is ahead. The little boy dies. No sorrow is like that of a mother who loses a child. She takes him to the man of God. Trouble is the time to go to church, not stay away. Her CONFIDENCE (vv. 22-37). Elisha's questions are for us today: "Is it well with thee? ... husband? ... child?" She gets her boy back!

PRAYER: "Lord, I claim my children for You."

SEPTEMBER 28

READING: 2 Kings 5

> *"Behold, I thought ... now I know ..." 2 Kings 5:11,15*

Elisha healing Naaman from leprosy is mentioned by our Lord (Luke 4:27). Elisha reminds us of Jesus. He had time for people. Follow the miracle. Naaman's DISEASE (vv. 1-7). Naaman was chief of staff of a foreign army. Great in many ways. One statement ruins the picture: " ... but he was a leper." (v. 1). Sin ruins the picture. But there is a prophet who has the solution for leprosy. Faithful preachers have the solution to the sin problem. His name is Jesus. Elisha's DIRECTIVE (vv. 8-15). Dipping seven times in a muddy river sounds foolish and trite. The answer is simple, but effective. Do what God says. Naaman goes from "I thought" to "I know." People have their own idea of how to deal with the leprosy of sin. When you take God's remedy, you can know.

PRAYER: "Lord Jesus, I am glad I can say, 'One thing I know'."

SEPTEMBER 29

READING: 2 Kings 20

"... I have heard thy prayer, I have seen thy tears ..." 2 Kings 20:5

Hezekiah was one of Judah's great kings (2 Kings 18:1-7). He was the good son of a bad father. But, the godly aren't free from problems. And mistakes. His SICKNESS (vv. 1-4). God's message to him is to the point and attention getting: "Set thine house in order; for thou shalt die, and not live." What do you do with that kind of message? The only thing you can. You pray (vv. 2-3). His SIGN (vv. 5-11). There are times when God hears and heals. His SORROW (v. 12). Then Hezekiah makes a bad mistake (v. 15). The same people who were given the grand tour of his treasures would one day carry it all away to Babylon. Answered prayer and healing don't prevent us from making mistakes. God must be followed daily.

PRAYER: *"Lord, today I understand I must walk with You each day."*

SEPTEMBER 30

READING: 2 Chronicles 34

"... while he was yet young, he began to seek after the God of David ..."
2 Chronicles 34:3

Josiah was the last godly king of Judah. He came to the throne and to the Lord as an 8 year old. In this chapter we see him CLEANSING God's LAND (vv. 3-7). He does all he can do to bring about revival to his people. But, you can't make people serve the Lord. REPAIRING God's HOUSE (vv. 8-13). Today our churches are in need of spiritual repair. We need to undergird the basics of prayer, teaching and preaching God's Word, winning the lost and fellowshipping with each other. FINDING God's BOOK (vv. 14-28). God's Word is lost in many modern churches. We need to go back to the Bible. GATHERING God's PEOPLE (vv. 29-33). The people are gathered and the Word is read. And the people commit to follow it.

PRAYER: *"Send us such a revival, O Lord."*

October

PERSONALS.

Do you read somebody else's mail? You will this month! For our devotions we will be reading letters by and to New Testament people—Paul; Timothy; Titus; Philemon; Peter. Actually, the Holy Spirit inspired them for us as well. And he gets personal!

OCTOBER 1

READING: 1 Timothy 1:1-11

"Unto Timothy, my own son in the faith" 1 Timothy 1:2

Paul the older preacher is writing Timothy the younger preacher. What a wonderful relationship was theirs. No evidence of a generation gap is to be found between them. Christ should bring believers of all ages together in the faith. Paul's words to this young preacher teach us a lot about the care of young converts. GREETED (vv. 1-2). Timothy was Paul's son in the faith. We can only imagine how it came about. Through a sermon? Through personal witnessing in the home? Converts are won in many ways. GUARDED (vv. 3-7). Timothy is to remain on duty in Ephesus. Converts must not be captured by false teachers. GUIDED (vv. 8-11). "Sound doctrine," which means healthy or wholesome teaching. Bad food makes one sick. Bad teaching is detrimental to spiritual health. Wholesome Gospel teaching is the remedy for spiritual sickness (v. 11).

PRAYER: "Lord, may I help a young convert."

OCTOBER 2

READING: 1 Timothy 1:12-20

" ... but I obtained mercy ..." 1 Timothy 1:13

Do you have a personal testimony? Can you give it? Paul gives his in today's verses. We learn the ingredients of an effective testimony. A THANKFUL SERVANT (vv. 12-14). Paul never got over what Jesus did for him. Nor should we. He chose me! He trusts me! He enabled me! Mercy means God didn't give us what we deserve. Grace means God gives us what we don't deserve. A FAITHFUL SAYING (vv. 15-16). These faithful sayings are scattered throughout Paul's pastoral epistles (1 Timothy 1:15; 3:1; 4:9; 2 Timothy 2:11; Titus 3:8). This one is about the Savior and sinners. A RESOURCEFUL SAVIOR (v. 17). As Paul reaches the climax of his testimony his heart bursts forth into a doxology of praise. And so does ours. Doxology follows true conversion.

PRAYER: "Today, dear Savior, my personal testimony causes me to rejoice in Your great salvation again. Glory! Hallelujah!"

OCTOBER 3

READING: 1 Timothy 2

"I will therefore that men pray every where ..." 1 Timothy 2:8

The importance of beginning your day reading the Bible and praying is everywhere taught in the Bible. Prayer. Don't leave home without it. Paul gives young Timothy a tremendous teaching on prayer. The FIRST call to Prayer: the BASICS (vv. 1-2). All types of prayer are mentioned. "Supplications"—requests for personal needs. "Prayers"—prayers of devotion to God. "Intercessions"—asking for the needs of others. "Giving of thanks"—thanking God for answered prayer. The FURTHER call to Prayer: the SPECIFICS (vv. 3-7). We are given some idea of the specific things for which we should pray. And, there is a tremendous truth that God desires all to be saved (v. 4). The FINAL call to Prayer: the DYNAMICS (v. 8). "Lifting up holy hands" indicates expecting to receive the answer from heaven! Bow you knee; lift your hands.

PRAYER: *"Now, Lord, I bow my knees to You in holy prayer."*

OCTOBER 4

READING: 1 Timothy 3

" ... that thou mayest know how thou oughtest to behave thyself in the house of God ..." 1 Timothy 3:15

The world looks on to see the behavior of God's people. Here are some guidelines for our behavior in the house of God. The LEADERS (vv. 1-7). Bishops are also called pastors and elders in the New Testament. The offices are interchangeable. God expects those who are in the position of spiritual oversight to meet certain qualifications. Perfection is not indicated, but a sincere desire to behave in a way that will be a good testimony. The HELPERS (vv. 8-13). God ordained that deacons be spiritual men who assist the pastors in the work of the church. They are to meet standards of behavior as well. The MEMBERS (vv. 14-16). The standards of conduct are high for all the members in God's church. If church members don't behave and beautify the truth, who will?

PRAYER: *"Lord, help me to behave myself today!"*

OCTOBER 5

READING: 1 Timothy 4:1-11

" ... in the latter times ..." 1 Timothy 4:1

The last days just before the return of Christ will be apostate. It will be a time of turning away from the Word of God by the professing church. Paul gives several needed words for believers. A word of CAUTION (vv. 1-5). "Seducing spirits and doctrines of demons" points to the satanic origin of last days doctrine and deception. Believers must be careful they do not fall for these Biblically contrary teachings. A word of COUNSEL (vv. 6-8). Believers need to be "nourished up," that is constantly feeding on the spiritual food provided in the Bible. And, "exercising" to be more godly. As athletes train the body, believers must train their souls to godliness. A word of COMMITMENT (vv. 9-11). Another faithful saying. And, a statement that Jesus is the Savior for all potentially, and the Savior actually of those who believe.

PRAYER: "Lord, help me to beware of apostate teaching."

OCTOBER 6

READING: 1 Timothy 4:12-16

"Let no man despise thy youth ..." 1 Timothy 4:12

When did you come to Christ? Surveys indicate most do at an early age. Timothy came to Christ in the days of his youth. Young believers need today's timely encouragement. The PATTERN of your life (v. 12). Even young Christians can be an example in several ways. By your words and lifestyle you can show others what a Christian life is to look like. The PROGRESS of your life (vv. 13-15). "Profiting" carries the idea of a way being cut ahead of an advancing army. Are you making progress as a believer? "Give attention to reading …" the Word of God. The PURPOSE of your life (v. 16). "Save thyself" refers not to soul salvation, but to living a fruitful worthwhile life. You can also be a winner of those who "hear thee." Young believer, be an example!

PRAYER: "Dear God, I want to be an example for others to follow."

OCTOBER 7

READING: 1 Timothy 5

"Honor widows that are widows indeed." 1 Timothy 5:3

The church is made up of people. We are in the people business. As a church made up of people we are compared to a family. The church must have concern for the members of the family. The TOTAL family (vv. 1-2). Fathers; brothers; mothers; sisters. Family! Each member, whatever age or station, must be treated with Christian respect and courtesy. Note how respectful Paul is. "Entreat" carries that idea of gentle appeal Whether old or young, each member of the church family must be accepted and loved. The SPECIAL family (vv. 3-16). The early church had a widow's list. The first responsibility was their immediate family. Then, the church was to assist them. The widow's ultimate help is the Lord (vv. 5-7). Her immediate help is from the church (vv. 9-15). May she be cared for by her church.

PRAYER: "Lord, the widows are precious to you and to me."

OCTOBER 8

READING: 1 Timothy 6

" ... the living God, who giveth us richly all things to enjoy ..." 1 Timothy 6:17

Are you rich? I've met few who admit they are. But, think again. Are you rich? Three levels of riches are found in today's devotion. MATERIAL riches (vv. 17-19). There are some who are "rich in this world." Material riches may be abused. They may be "trusted." This is an uncertain trust. Never depend on anything earthly. Material riches may be used. You may enjoy them (v. 17) and employ them (vv. 18-19). SPIRITUAL riches (vv. 20-21a). The second level gets better. Believers have a precious treasure, referred to as "thy trust" (v. 20). This is the message of the Gospel (See 1 Timothy 1:11). What glorious riches! ETERNAL riches (v. 21b). The third level is even better! "Eternal life!" How rich are you? Do you have the eternal riches of God's eternal grace and glory?

PRAYER: "Lord, I am rich indeed."

OCTOBER 9

READING: 2 Timothy 1

" ... *stir up the gift of God ...*" 2 Timothy 1:6

As far as we know this is Paul's farewell letter. It consists of his last words to the young preacher, Timothy, and the Holy Spirit's words to us. Paul is in prison. He will never be a free man again. But, his heart is turned toward others. The PEOPLE (vv. 1-2). He mentions himself, Timothy and the Lord Jesus. So, this letter is written by Paul, to Timothy, about Jesus! O how Paul loved Jesus. Reading what he says about Jesus causes us to love Jesus more and more. The PRAYER (vv. 3-5). Paul's written prayers are high water marks in his letters. Do you have a prayer list? Who will you pray for today? The PLEA (vv. 6-7). Paul says "stir up the gift of God ..." We must keep the fire of our devotion to Christ burning brightly.

PRAYER: *"Lord, today I stir up my soul by the poker of Your Word."*

OCTOBER 10

READING: 2 Timothy 2

" ... *he shall be a vessel unto honor ...*" 2 Timothy 2:21

The Bible uses many figures of speech to explain what it means to be saved and to serve Jesus Christ. Here, we are like vessels in a great house. As one of the Lord's vessels we must live a certain kind of life. A DEDICATED life (vv. 20-21). Each household has different kinds of vessels. Magnificent silver serving bowls; wood bowls; crystal goblets; clay pots. Each of us should be on display for God's glory. "Vessels unto honor" is the goal. A DETERMINED life (vv. 22-23). There are some dangers that keep us from being useful vessels for the Lord Jesus. Flee them! A DISCIPLINED life (vv. 24-26). To be disciplined in attitude (v. 24) and activity (vv. 25-26) will help us to be vessels that will honor the Lord.

PRAYER: *"Lord, wherever I am placed, help me be a vessel that will bring honor and glory to You."*

OCTOBER 11

READING: 2 Timothy 3:1-9

> *" ... in the last days perilous times shall come." 2 Timothy 3:1*

Our devotional today gives another description of days of apostasy. Before Jesus returns certain moral, social and spiritual conditions will snowball. PREDICTED (v. 1). In a sense the last days includes the time from Christ's birth until His return. But, there will be some last days of the last days. They will be "perilous," that is, difficult to deal with. PICTURED (vv. 2-5). The lifestyle of society will be like an ugly, gaping sore. Nineteen characteristics of last days society are catalogued. It is an accurate description of what we see in our culture today. PROMOTED (vv. 6-9). Such immorality worms its way in. This is done through TV shows, movies, literature, etc. In dangerous days isn't it wonderful to have a Savior? He gives us strength to resist the pressures of these apostate days.

PRAYER: "Lord, help me not to adopt the ways of an apostate society."

OCTOBER 12

READING: 2 Timothy 3:10-17

> *"All Scripture is given by inspiration of God ..." 2 Timothy 3:16*

In apostate days such as ours we need a book to guide us in all matters of faith and practice. God has given us just such a book! The Bible is the believer's textbook and guidebook. Its INSPIRATION (v. 16a). Not part of, nor most of, but all of Scripture is God-breathed. The Bible owes its origin and contents to the Holy Breath of God (2 Peter 1:21). Therefore, whatever the Bible says about any matter is true. Its INFORMATION (v.16b). The Bible is "profitable." This means it is useful. It is useful for our forward ("doctrine"), false ("reproof"), faltering ("correction") and first ("instruction") steps. Its INTENTION (v. 17). "Complete" and "furnished" doesn't mean sinless perfection. It means fitted and fully equipped for the voyage of life.

PRAYER: "Lord, today I open the book You have given me. Teach me Thy ways, O Lord."

OCTOBER 13

READING: 2 Timothy 4:1-8

" ... the time of my departure is at hand" 2 Timothy 4:6

These are the final words of the old preacher, Paul, to young Timothy. He is getting ready to head home. Tradition says Paul was beheaded in Rome. How does he view his emminent death? What about his present? PREPARATION (v. 6). "I am now ready ..." Death for Paul is like an offering and a departure. Like an offering on the altar or a tent pulled up and moving on, Paul stands ready. What about his past? COMPLETION (v. 7). He is like a wrestler who has "fought a good fight", a runner who has "finished my course", a banker who has "kept the faith." What about the future? ANTICIPATION (v. 8). Using another athletic picture Paul sees himself winning the race and being called up to receive the victor's crown of victory. What a way to go!

PRAYER: "Lord Jesus, if today is my last day, may I be ready and looking heavenward."

OCTOBER 14

READING: 2 Timothy 4:9-22

"Do thy diligence to come before winter." 2 Timothy 4:21

There is urgency in Paul's words as he asks Timothy to come to see him. Why "before winter?" Because the weather may overtake Timothy and death may overtake him. His words speak to us today. Life's BREVITY ("winter"). The physical world has its seasons. So does the spiritual world. Spring, summer, fall and winter. Childhood, youth, adulthood, and old age. Winter is coming. Life's OPPORTUNITY ("before"). Opportunity is a favorable juncture of circumstances. Some come only one time. Take them or they are gone forever. Life's URGENCY ("come"). God joins Paul in the use of the word "come." It is the great word of Gospel invitation. People need to come to Christ while there is still time. Did Timothy make it on time? We can only speculate. Have you done what God wants you to do? That is the more important question today.

PRAYER: "Lord Jesus, may I not tarry, but 'come before winter'."

OCTOBER 15

READING: **Titus 1**

" ... whose mouths must be stopped ..." Titus 1:11

Paul had a way with young preachers. He wrote Timothy. He wrote a letter to another one, Titus, the young pastor in Crete (vv. 4-5). This young pastor must be on guard against the false teachers. We learn how false teaching is DISSEMENATED (vv. 10-11). False teachers think they are smarter than the Word of God. They are "vain talkers." Their words may sound impressive, but it is idle chatter. They are often out for money ("filthy lucre"). How it is DIRECTED (vv. 12-14). False teachers direct their message toward man's tendency to evil (v. 12) and error (v. 14). How it is DETECTED (vv. 15-16). How do you tell if teaching is bad? Give it the test of character (v. 15). What kind of people does it produce? Give it the test of conduct (v. 16). Watch out for the garbage peddlers!

PRAYER: "Lord, today may I guard against the false teachers."

OCTOBER 16

READING: **Titus 2**

"For the grace of God ... hath appeared to all men." Titus 2:11

John Newton wrote the amazing hymn, *Amazing Grace*. Properly understood the only word for grace is amazing. It is amazing because of what it brings. SALVATION (v. 11). God has made salvation available for all. He provided it through the substitutionary death of Jesus Christ (v. 14). EDUCATION (v. 12). Grace is a wonderful teacher. When saved, a person enters into Grace School. Grace teaches us what not to do ("…denying…"). It also teaches us what to do ("… we should live…"). ANTICIPATION (v. 13). Grace gives us a great anticipation. We are awaiting "that blessed hope." One day we shall witness the "appearance of the glory." Grace teaches us; glory thrills us. Whatever begins in grace always ends in glory. Grace is the root; glory is the fruit. By grace one day we shall look upon the glory. "Amazing grace, how sweet the sound …"

PRAYER: "Dear heavenly Father, thank You for amazing grace."

OCTOBER 17

READING: Titus 3

"But after that the kindness and love of God ... appeared ..." Titus 3:4

Our devotion today summarizes the whole Christian life. It tells us what we were, what we are, and what we shall be. Our PAST life (v. 3). Not a pretty picture, is it? We should never forget where we came from and what we used to be. But, we don't need to dwell on the past. Our PRESENT life (vv. 4-6). This is a corner verse in Scripture. Things looked bad. "But!" What a contrast. We are now saved because of what God the Father (v. 4), God the Son (v. 5a), and God the Holy Spirit (v. 5b) have done for us. The Father thought it; The Son brought it; The Spirit wrought it! Our PROSPECTIVE life (v. 7). Now we look to our future with hope. Hope is not something uncertain. Bible hope is confident expectation based upon the promises of God.

PRAYER: *"Lord, thank You for such a full salvation."*

OCTOBER 18

READING: Philemon

" ... put that on mine account." Philemon 18

The brief letter to Philemon is a Gospel masterpiece. Philemon: A REFRESHING SAINT (vv. 4-7). This wealthy Christian was won to Christ by Paul. It is refreshing to see a believer whose life reaches Godward ("faith") and manward ("love") (v. 5). Onesimus: A RECLAIMED SLAVE (vv. 8-16). Onesimus was Philemon's runaway slave. But, Paul led him to Christ in prison! Now, he sends him back, not as a slave, but as a brother in Christ. He who was once unprofitable is now profitable. Salvation has a way of doing that, doesn't it? Paul: A REDEMPTIVE SOULWINNER (vv. 17-21). As Paul opens his heart, we see Jesus there. Paul expresses the beautiful Bible truth of substitution. Our sin debt was placed on Christ at the cross and He paid it in full. Yes, "the old account was settled long ago."

PRAYER: *"Lord Jesus, thank You for taking my sin debt and paying it in full."*

OCTOBER 19

READING: James 1

"Blessed is the man that endureth temptation ..." James 1:12

James, the half brother of our Lord, gives us practical, helpful words concerning troubles that come in our life. The FACT of trouble (v. 2). Note he didn't say, "if." He said "when" troubles come. Trouble is a part of life. We really aren't prepared for his words, "count it all joy ..." The word, count, is a banking term. Trouble may seem a liability. But, James knows before it is over, it will be in the asset column. The FUNCTION of trouble (vv. 3-4). Trouble has a 3-fold function in our life. Trouble tests us. Satan tempts us to bring out the worst in us. God tests us to bring out the best in us. Trouble teaches us. "Worketh patience." We aren't born with a lot of patience. Trouble transforms us. "Let" means allow trouble to do its work.

PRAYER: "Lord, today, I know You have a purpose for my troubles."

OCTOBER 20

READING: James 2

" ... have not the faith ... with respect of persons." James 2:1

James takes us to church. There is no place for snobbishness or partiality in the church of the Lord Jesus Christ. A PROHIBITION (v. 1). "Respect of persons" means to show favoritism to someone because of riches or popularity. Don't do it!, says James. An ILLUSTRATION (vv. 2-4). A rich man and a poor man come into the service. A short-sighted usher shows partiality on the basis of the superficial ("apparel ... raiment ... clothing ..."), the material (riches versus poverty) and the temporal. He should have looked beyond what his eyes could see to eternal values. An APPLICATION (vv. 5-13). Now comes the sermon. James says partiality is a sin. We must remember that the way we treat people will be one of the ways we will be examined by the Lord.

PRAYER: "Lord, help me to love and respect people, regardless of their state in life. Help me to be impartial, like You are."

OCTOBER 21

READING: James 3

"Even so the tongue is a little member ..." James 3:5

Today, a little lesson about a subject that is in everybody's mouth. The tongue! Using a series of word pictures James shows us the nature of the tongue. The DIRECTIVE nature of the tongue (vv. 3-4). It is like a small bit, directing a large horse. It is like a small rudder, directing a huge ship. The DESTRUCTIVE nature of the tongue (vv. 5-8). The tongue can burn like a fire. It can be as unruly as a wild animal. Like a poisonous snake, it can strike, deposit its deadly poison, and slither away. The DECEPTIVE nature of the tongue (vv. 9-12). Contrary to nature, the tongue can give forth sweet and bitter water. It can produce widely differing fruit. Though we can't control our tongue, Jesus can!

PRAYER: "Lord, today may my tongue speak no words that do not honor You. May I use my tongue to sing Your praises."

OCTOBER 22

READING: James 4

" ... know ye not that the friendship of the world is enmity with God?" James 4:4

When Christians flirt with this world we are like a person being unfaithful to his/her mate. In blunt, pointed language James sets forth the tragedy of a worldly life. The SINFULNESS of it (v. 4). To be worldy is a sin against love ("adulterers"). It is a sin against light ("know ye not ... ?"). And, it is a sin against liberty ("will be"). The SERIOUSNESS of it (vv. 5-6a). We offend the Holy Spirit who dwells within us and jealously longs for our total devotion. The SENSELESSNESS of it (v. 6b). Worldliness will involve you in a war with God. And, you can't win it. God will frustrate your aims and defeat your plans. Better to turn from this world and devote our life totally to faithful love for Christ.

PRAYER: "Lord Jesus, may I not flirt with this world today, but love You supremely."

OCTOBER 23

READING: James 5

> "... the coming of the Lord draweth nigh." *James 5:8*

As the days get darker and times of trouble come, the truth of the return of Christ becomes precious. James encourages us to "be patient...unto the coming of the Lord." (v. 7). Around this truth James tells us how to make it until then. Let the truth that Jesus is coming again EXCITE us ("draweth nigh... at doors"). This truth should stir us to a new enthusiasm in our living and our witnessing. Let it EXAMINE us ("patient ... stablish your hearts"). As we await His return we ask ourselves, am I strong in heart? Am I sweet in spirit ("Grudge not ...")? Am I sound in words ("swear not ...")? Let this truth ENCOURAGE us (vv. 10-11). What an encouragement Job is! Though Job didn't understand all he was experiencing, he trusted that God had a purpose. Let Job encourage us.

PRAYER: *"Today, Lord Jesus I lift my heart and say, 'Even so, come!' "*

OCTOBER 24

READING: 1 Peter 1

> "... which things the angels desire to look into." *1 Peter 1:12*

A letter from the Big Fisherman! Peter gives us great words of hope based upon the salvation we have in Christ. Through his first letter he keeps coming back to the spectacular truth of salvation. Prophetic EXPECTATION (vv. 10-12a). Old Testament prophets were inspired to see the coming of Christ. They were given more than they understood. Apostolic PROCLAMATION (v. 12b). The Apostles proclaimed the good news of the death, burial and resurrection of Christ. We have the same good news to share with our world. Suffering and glory go together. The sufferings of the cross led to the glory of the resurrection. Angelic FASCINATION (v. 12c). Angels can't share salvation; but they do study it. Angels don't receive salvation; but they do rejoice when people do. How spectacular! And it's all about you.

PRAYER: *"Lord Jesus, thank You for Your great salvation is meant for me and all who will come to Christ."*

OCTOBER 25

READING: 1 Peter 2

" ... because Christ suffered for us ..." 1 Peter 2:21

In the midst of this chapter that shows us how to handle suffering is a moving description of the cross of Christ. The VIRTUOUS nature of Christ's cross (vv. 22-23). The point here is that Jesus didn't deserve death on the cross. But He suffered sinlessly ("did no sin") and silently ("no guile"). The VICARIOUS nature of His cross (v. 24). Though He had no sin, He bore our sins in His body on the cross. What a load Christ bore when He carried the sins of the world to the tree. The VICTORIOUS nature of His cross (v. 25). People are like straying sheep. Lost, aimless and helpless without God are we. Christ, the Shepherd, sought us and returned us back to God. It is good to know that the Shepherd is interested in that one lost sheep (See Luke 15).

PRAYER: *"Thank You, Lord Jesus, for finding me."*

OCTOBER 26

READING: 1 Peter 3

"Who is gone into heaven, and is on the right hand of God ..." 1 Peter 3:22

In the midst of some verses of difficult understanding, one message is quite clear—Jesus wins! Jesus wins because he conquered On the CROSS (v. 18). He was the "just" suffering for the "unjust." And in so doing He brought us to God. Jesus wins! He conquered In the COFFIN (vv. 18c-21). The tomb certainly looked like a defeat for Jesus. But He was made alive by the Holy Spirit. Jesus wins! He conquered Through the CLOUDS (v. 22). His conquest not only was assured in the regions below, it was recognized in regions above. In His ascension He returned to heaven as Master, Forerunner and Victor. Jesus wins! Now He is seated on the throne in heaven. Jesus wins! And so do we!

PRAYER: *"Lord Jesus, how good to know that You conquered. And, thank You that I am more than a conquerer because I share in Your victory."*

OCTOBER 27

READING: 1 Peter 4

"Yet if any man suffer as a Christian, let him not be ashamed ..."
1 Peter 4:16

Today's devotion in a nutshell: If you are a suffering Christian, don't be surprised. Suffering is a part of the plan. And, suffering is the pathway to glory. There are several aspects of suffering in the Christian life. The OBJECT of your suffering (vv. 12-14). Suffering purifies you (v. 12), identifies you (v. 13a) and glorifies you (vv. 13-14). The OBLIGATION of your suffering (vv. 15-16). Be sure your suffering is not because of your own sin. Some suffering is deserved (v. 15); some is derived (v. 16). The OVERVIEW of your suffering (vv. 17-18). Suffering is also a part of the overall process of God's judgment process. Don't try to understand it. Just remember, suffering is a part of the plan. The OUTCOME of your suffering (v. 19). Commit it to God and keep on doing right.

PRAYER: *"Father, I'm glad You have a plan."*

OCTOBER 28

READING: 1 Peter 5

"To Him be glory and dominion for ever and ever." 1 Peter 5:11

Peter compares the Christian life to a pilgrimage (See 2:11; 1:17). A pilgrim is on a journey homeward. The Pilgrim's ATTITUDE (vv. 5-7). We should be humble in our attitude toward one another. We should wear it like a slave's apron. We must also be humble in our attitude toward our heavenly Father. When we humble ourselves, God will ultimately exalt us. In due time. The Pilgrim's ADVERSARY (vv. 8-9). Pilgrims have enemies along the way home. Our adversary, the devil, is like a roaring lion. But, the good news is that we can "resist" him. Victory through Christ is assured. The Pilgrim's ARRIVAL (vv.10-11). One day the journey will be over. There will be glory awaiting us! Whatever begins in grace always ends in glory. Glory is a Person, but also a place. Saints and angels will announce, Welcome home, Pilgrim!

PRAYER: *"Father, I'm marching toward Gloryland."*

OCTOBER 29

READING: 2 Peter 1

" ... to them that have obtained like precious faith ..." 2 Peter 1:1

Peter sets before us "precious faith." Faith that is the genuine article. Peter mentions a lot of "precious things" (1 Peter 1:7; 1 Peter 1:19; 1 Peter 2:4, 6; 1 Peter 2:7; 2 Peter 1:4). Precious faith means we are saved by a Divine PERSON (vv. 1-2). Knowing Jesus brings God's grace and peace into our life. Grace makes us right with God; peace makes us right with others. A Divine POWER (v. 3). God gives us power to have life and godliness. And it comes through our knowledge of the Lord Jesus. A Divine PROMISE (v. 4). Oh the precious promises saving faith brings into our life. How great are these promises. How precious are they. The worth of a promise is dependant upon the character and ability of the one making it. God will keep His promises.

PRAYER: *"Lord, thank You for precious faith."*

OCTOBER 30

READING 2 Peter 2

"The dog is turned to his own vomit again ..." 2 Peter 2:22

I hope you aren't reading this devotion just before your breakfast! Might make you sick. Peter gives us a lengthy portrait of false teachers. Their PRONOUNCEMENTS are false (v. 18). Their words are not only empty ("vanity"), but they are erroneous ("error"). Their PROMISES are false (v. 19). They promise liberty, but what they do is bring people into bondage. Their PROFESSIONS are false (vv. 20-22). False teachers are pictured as dogs and hogs. They give evidence of their true nature because they return to their previous pollutions. A dog is still a dog. A pig is still a pig. God's people are sheep. Each will eventually return to his father's house. Good news. Jesus can take dogs and hogs and make them sheep!

PRAYER: *"Lord Jesus, I thank You that I am one of Your sheep today. Help me not to act like a dog or a hog!"*

OCTOBER 31

READING: 2 Peter 3

> *"Looking for and hasting unto the coming of the day of God ..."*
> *2 Peter 3:12*

Today is man's day. God will have His. Today people have the opportunity to come to Christ (2 Corinthians 6:2). Let's look at the day of God as it relates to several realities. The CREATION (vv. 10-11a). If this creation is going to be dissolved, a person is a fool to choose it over the Lord Jesus. The CHRISTIAN (vv. 11b-12). The anticipation of the consummation of all things calls for believers to live holy lives. Let us so live that we will be glad to see Jesus come. The CONSUMMATION (v. 13). Three worlds are in view in this chapter: The PAST world (v. 6); the PRESENT world (v. 7); and the PROMISED world (v. 13). The only way to get into the new world is to have a new birth.

PRAYER: *"Lord Jesus, I am living in light of Your day."*

November

MAJORING ON THE MINORS.

The minor prophets are minor in size, but certainly not minor in message. There are some major messages for us in these prophetic books. We will major on these minors in November.

NOVEMBER 1

READING: Hosea 1

"Go, take unto thee a wife of whoredoms ..." Hosea 1:2

Everyone enjoys a love story. The Bible tells the greatest love story ever told (John 3:16). Hosea has a love story for us. He has been called the prophet of love; or the broken heart. The strange instruction to marry Gomer tells the story of God's great love for fallen mankind. The SETTING (v. 1). Hosea dates the time when he preached. It was a time of material prosperity, but spiritual promiscuity. The STORYLINE (v. 2). Modernize the story: A young preacher boy needs a wife. God tells him to marry Gomer. But, she's a prostitute! Hosea's marriage will become a parable of God's love for unfaithful sinners. The SHAME (vv. 3-11). Soon after the marriage, children are born: Jezreel (God scatters); Loruhamah (no pity); Laommi (no kin of mine). God uses Hosea's marriage to tell the greatest love story ever told.

PRAYER: "Lord, I'm amazed You love me, sinner that I am."

NOVEMBER 2

READING: Hosea 2:1-13

"For their mother hath played the harlot ..." Hosea 2:5

There's trouble at the preacher's house! What God said is true. Hosea's wife, Gomer, is a prostitute. God is using Hosea's marriage tragedy to teach spiritual truth. Her DEPARTURE (vv. 1-5). Off she goes with her lovers. She thinks her lovers give her what she needs (v. 5). Who gets credit for your blessings (v. 8)? Her DESPAIR (vv. 6-8). She is passed down from lover to lover. When you wander away from the Lord, there is trouble every step of the way. Her DESPERATION (vv. 9-12). Gomer hits the bottom. Sooner or later that is what happens when you leave the Lord. Her necessities collapse (v. 9), her festivities cease (v. 11) and her anxieties come (vv. 12-13). The greatest sin of all is sin against love. How is your love life between you and Jesus?

PRAYER: "Lord Jesus, forgive me for sinning against Your great love for me."

NOVEMBER 3

READING: Hosea 2:14-3:5

" ... so I bought her for myself ..." Hosea 3:2

Hosea has a broken heart. He is trying to be a father and a mother to the children, and they aren't even his! He teaches us what sin does. Now, he will show us what love does. Love RESPONDS (vv. 2:14-23). Note the repetition of "I will." Steps will be taken for Hosea to buy Gomer back. God still loves us in spite of our sin. Love REDEEMS (3:1-2). What Hosea does for Gomer pictures what God does for us. We are sought by love (3:1) and we are bought by love (3:2). "He sought me and He bought me with His redeeming blood." Love RESTORES (3:3-5). Hosea says to Gomer, From now on you're living with me. Remember, it is not Gomer who sought Hosea; it is Hosea who sought Gomer. Get the message?

PRAYER: *"Lord, thank You for seeking and finding me."*

NOVEMBER 4

READING: Hosea 4

" ... there is no truth, nor mercy, nor knowledge of God in the land."
Hosea 4:1

Hosea 1-3 tells of Hosea's marriage. Hosea 4-14 gives his messages. In 4:1 we suddenly find ourselves in a courtroom. God is the prosecuting attorney. Sin not only breaks God's heart. It outrages His holiness. The CHARGES (vv. 1-3). The Lord gives a bill of particulars. Charge after charge is hurled at God's people. He builds a devastating case. God indeed has our number. The CAUSES (vv. 6-17). What has caused such outrage? Ignorance (vv. 6-8), idolatry (vv. 12-13), and immorality (v. 4:12b) all play a part. These pictures and questions cause us to ask, how lasting, how deep, how strong, how serious, how dependable is our devotion to God? But, there is hope! Hosea 6:1-3 shows the way back to God.

PRAYER: *"Lord, I have wandered from You. Help me today to return to You for Your healing."*

NOVEMBER 5

READING: Hosea 8

> *" ... they have sown the wind, and they shall reap the whirlwind ..."*
> *Hosea 8:7*

Hosea discusses Israel's pollution (Hosea 4-7) and their punishment (Hosea 8-10). What do events that happened centuries ago have to do with us today? The spiritual principles that applied then still apply today. God's physical laws of the universe are unchanging. We don't break them; we violate them and they break us. The same is true of God's spiritual laws. Hosea declares, Judgment is on the way! Looks at its characteristics. SUDDEN (v. 1). Like a trumpet of alarm, a series of announcements of God's sudden judgments are listed. SWIFT (v. 1). God's judgment will be as swift as an eagle. Assyria was about to swoop down and destroy Israel. Our sin makes us wonder if judgment is not swiftly coming. SURE (v. 7). God's judgment operates on the law of sowing and reaping. And, we always reap more than we sow.

PRAYER: *"Lord, may we repent before judgment falls."*

NOVEMBER 6

READING: Hosea 11

> *"I drew them with cords of a man, with bands of love ..." Hosea 11:4*

Hosea doesn't end on a gloomy note. He has discussed Israel's pollution (Hosea 4-7), its punishment (Hosea 8-10). Now, he speaks for its pardon (Hosea 11-14). God's persistent love permeates these messages. His love EXPLAINED (vv. 1-7). God surveys His past dealings with them. His past love is a promise of His present love. His love EXCLAIMED (vv. 8-9). The depth and pathos of God's love shines through in verse 8. God is saying, My heart is moved to its depths for you. Here is the dilemma of Deity. God is just and must punish sin; He is love and wants to spare the sinner. The dilemma was solved at the cross! His love EXTENDED (vv. 10-12). Though we deserve His wrath and tremble, God is longsuffering to us.

PRAYER: *"I praise You today, Holy God, for Your Calvary love."*

NOVEMBER 7

READING: Joel 1:1-2:11

" ... for the day of the Lord cometh, for it is nigh at hand ..." Joel 2:1

We don't know a lot about Joel. He appears suddenly, speaks his message and then is gone. His message concerns national tragedy. Two days are in view: the day of locusts and the day of the Lord. The PRESENT FAMINE: IMMEDIATE JUDGMENT (Joel 1). Joel says God will send an invasion of locusts upon the land as a sign of God's displeasure. What are the locusts today? Technology; economic structures; etc. The PROSPECTIVE FOES: IMMINENT JUDGMENT (2:1-11). Now that Joel has our attention, he points us to the future. The locusts merely prelude something far worse. Now comes an army of human soldiers. The locusts morph into a human army right before our eyes. The reference is to the Assyrian invasion. What are the locust-like armies we face today? A culture that captures the minds and hearts of a godless people.

PRAYER: "Lord, are the locusts coming?"

NOVEMBER 8

READING: Joel 2:12-27

"I will restore to you the years that the locust hath eaten ..." Joel 2:25

Joel speaks against the backdrop of national disaster. When disaster strikes, it is a call to repentance. God gives a PRESCRIPTION: You REPENT (2:12-17). Repentance is not a pleasant prescription. It is a rugged process. When we truly repent of sin our mind will abhor it, our heart will abominate it and our will will abandon it. But, it is the only way to avert God's judgment upon sin. God gives a PROMISE: I will RESTORE (vv. 18-27). God promises to restore "the years the locust hath eaten." What a promise! Do you think it is too late to repair the damage sin has caused in your life, and recover lost ground? It isn't. God can give you back what you would have had if the locusts caused by sin had not come. God can restore relationships and personal joy.

PRAYER: "Lord, thank You for Your restoring promise and power."

NOVEMBER 9

READING: Joel 2:28-3:21

> *"And it shall come to pass afterward, that I will pour out my Spirit upon all flesh ..." Joel 2:28*

Joel was a prophet. He was a forthteller of God's message to his day and a forteller of events for a future day. Joel gives the special promise of a great outpouring of the Holy Spirit. There are times in the Old Testament when a prophecy has a partial fulfillment; then a final fulfillment will come in the future. The SPIRIT will be poured OUT (2:28-32). Peter used this prophecy to explain to the people at Pentecost just what was happening (Acts 2:16-21). The JUDGMENT will be poured ON (3:1-16). There will be a time of great tribulation involving Israel and the nations. The BLESSING will be poured DOWN (3:17-21). In the Kingdom Age there will be millennial blessings. God's message for today?—(See Hosea 2:32.)

PRAYER: *"Lord Jesus, I am thankful today is the 'whosoever' day!"*

NOVEMBER 10

READING: Amos 7:10-17

> *" ... I am no prophet, neither am I a prophet's son ..." Amos 7:14*

Amos, the country preacher, comes to town. He was one of the Lord's prophets to a backslidden people. Prophets were the spiritual physicians of the day. They didn't cause the trouble; they put their finger on it. Dr. Ouch, if you please. Let's look at this preacher. His CREDENTIALS (1:1; 7:14-15). We don't know much about him. He was from a small town 10 miles south of Jerusalem. He was a herdsman and a gatherer of sycamore fruit. Perhaps his business trips north to the great market centers caused him to see the condition of the nations of the world. And, it made his blood boil. His CALL (7:12-15). He was not a prophet by profession. He was not in the long line of prophets. But, God told him, "Go, prophesy." And he did.

PRAYER: *"Lord, I am not a professional. Help me be Your messenger."*

NOVEMBER 11

READING: Amos 4

"Come to Bethel, and transgress; at Gilgal multiply transgression ..."
Amos 4:4

Amos wasn't the most tactful of preachers! He names the sins of the people. LUXURY (vv. 1-3). "Kine of Bashan" evidently refers to women in high society. Perhaps Amos was invited to speak to the Bashan Ladies' club. "Hear this, you fat heifers!" must have been a shocking introduction. They were enamored with their body, not their soul. To Amos they were just so many cows headed to slaughter. HYPOCRISY (vv. 4-5). Their religious worship was just another opportunity to sin. Every aspect of their worship was wrong. It can be dangerous to go to church. Do we attend in a spiritual condition to receive the Lord's blessings? OBSTINACY (vv. 6-13). God had sent a series of judgments, but His warning went unheeded. So, he says, "Prepare to meet thy God ..." Judgment is on the way.

PRAYER: *"Dear God, help me be an object of Your mercy in what I do today."*

NOVEMBER 12

READING: Amos 9

"In that day will I raise up the tabernacle of David that is fallen ..."
Amos 9:11

As Amos comes to the end of his prophecy the focus dramatically shifts from retribution to restoration, from judgment to hope. The judgment clouds roll away and the sun of restoration begins to shine. There is a better day coming. Amos sees there will be several restorations. DYNASTY (vv. 11-12). This prophecy has to do with the restoration of the royal family line of David. The tabernacle was indeed restored. God became flesh and "tabernacled" among us (John 1:14). When Christ returns and sits on the throne of David in the millennium (Luke 1:32-33) this will be completely fulfilled. PLENTY (vv. 13-14). There will be great abundance during the millennial reign of Christ. SECURITY (v. 15). God will take care of His own.

PRAYER: *"Dear Lord Jesus, You tabernacled among us in Your first coming. I look forward to Your second coming."*

NOVEMBER 13

READING: **Obadiah**

" ... as thou hast done, it shall be done unto thee ..." Obadiah 15

Obadiah tells the story of two boys, two nations and two cities. Petra and Jerusalem; Edom and Israel; Esau and Jacob. Actually, it is a family feud. Jacob and Esau were in the same family. It's also the story of the war between the flesh and the spirit in the life of a believer. DEFEAT for Edom (vv. 1-16). Judgment was on the way for Edom. War is coming. God will judge their pride (v. 3). God must judge the pride of our sinful flesh. It leads to sinful attitudes (v. 11) and actions (vv. 12-14). DELIVERANCE for Israel (vv. 17-24). God has future plans for Israel. The last verse is our haven of hope. God always blesses us when we allow the Holy Spirit to humble us and use us.

PRAYER: "Lord Jesus, judge the things in my flesh that keep me from yielding to the work of the Holy Spirit."

NOVEMBER 14

READING: Jonah 1

"But the Lord sent out a great wind into the sea ..." Jonah 1:4

To find and follow God's will for your life is vital. It is one thing to be uncertain about God's will and miss it. It is another to know it and refuse to do it. Jonah is the classic illustration of the latter. Jonah's FLIGHT (vv. 1-4). God tells Jonah to go west and he runs east. Everything seemed to work out. He "found the ship...paid the fare..." But, when you run from God it is always "down." And there's a storm coming (v. 4). The Sailor's FEAR (vv. 5-16). When the storm nearly cracks the ship in two, the sailors panic. What a sight! Pagan sailors praying and a backsliding prophet sleeping. The Lord's FISH (v. 17). Don't focus on the fish. Focus on the God who can "prepare" just what we need when we run from Him.

PRAYER: "Lord, today may I not run from You."

NOVEMBER 15

READING: Jonah 2

> *"When my soul fainted within me I remembered the Lord: and my prayer came in unto Thee ... " Jonah 2:7*

Run from God and you'll get in a "whale of a mess." Jonah lets us in on a very personal experience. See how God deals with him in the depths of the sea and in the depths of his soul. Isn't it ironic that when we get in trouble we run to the very one we've been running from? His DISTRESS (vv. 1-3, 5-6). His prayer is filled with references to Old Testament psalms. The Word of God and prayer go together. His DECISION (v. 4). This is the Old Testament equivalent of 1 John 1:9. His DELIVERANCE (vv. 7-10). Up from the bone-chilling cold of the sea the fish bursts toward the warmth of the sun, and spews out Jonah. Relief for the fish—Deliverance for Jonah.

PRAYER: "Lord, thank You for delivering me when I call on You."

NOVEMBER 16

READING: Jonah 3

> *"And the word of the Lord came unto Jonah the second time ..." Jonah 3:1*

God is the God of a second chance. Jonah has been running from God, to God and now he is ready to run for God. Jonah's PROCLAMATION (vv. 1-4). When we blow it we may think it is all over. It need not be. God used Jonah again. He will use you again. He delivers a strong message of God's judgment upon the city of Ninevah. It is a crisis message, but "40 days" gives a period of grace and opportunity. Nineveh's HUMILIATION (vv. 5-9). Nineveh's reaction is stunning. What Jonah least expected and never wanted happened. Nineveh repented. The miracle of conversion occurred from the lowliest houses up to the King's house. God's AFFIRMATION (v. 10). When the people turned God turned. God doesn't have to fulfill His punishments. He does have to fulfill His promises.

PRAYER: "Holy God, thank You for Your offer of mercy to me."

NOVEMBER 17

READING: Jonah 4

"And should I not spare Nineveh, that great city ... ?" Jonah 4:11

A great revival should make the prophet happy. But, it doesn't. Jonah is angry over the conversion of pagans. The DISTURBING COMPASSION (vv. 1-4). Jonah knew God quite well. He knew God would respond in mercy to the cries of a repentant people. Jonah wanted that compassion for his people, but not for Nineveh. He's piping hot. The PROBING LESSON (vv. 5-9). Jonah is happier over a gourd than the salvation of people. Too many of us get carried away with life's gourds. But God can send worms to eat up our gourds. The LINGERING QUESTION (v. 10-11). God's question reaches all the way to us. Is our comfort more important than God's compassion? Is the material more important than the spiritual? Is the temporal more important than the eternal? The book closes with a question. What is your answer?

PRAYER: *"Dear God, help me to love people more than my comforts."*

NOVEMBER 18

READING: Micah 5

" ... out of thee shall he come forth unto me that is to be ruler in Israel ..."
Micah 5:2

Micah was a prophet from a tiny town ("Moresheth") who talked about another tiny town ("Bethlehem"). He preached in turbulent times. The first and third parts of his book give the chilling news that Judgment (Micah 1-2) and justice (Micah 6-7) were coming. But, in the second part there was good news—Jesus is coming (Micah 3-5)! He would be born in the tiny town of Bethlehem. It was where the Savior would be born. His INCARNATION ("whose goings forth have been from of old"). The Savior would be the eternal God. His DURATION ("from everlasting"). Jesus stepped out of eternity into time; then He stepped back into eternity. His OCCUPATION ("ruler in Israel"). He is not only Savior; He is King of Kings and Lord of Lords!

PRAYER: *"Lord, I see why we sing 'O little town of Bethlehem ...'"*

NOVEMBER 19

READING: **Nahum 1**

"The Lord is good, a stronghold in the day of trouble ..." Nahum 1:7

Nahum's prophecy is the second Old Testament book about Nineveh. Jonah preached there and they repented. Time passes. Nahum wrote about them because wrath was now coming to the city. In Jonah God said, "I love them." In Nahum He says, "I must judge them." God draws the line on nations. Chapter one is a theology book teaching us about God. God is love; He is also holy. Nahum teaches us about the other side of God's character. The Lord's PATIENCE (vv. 1-3a). Three words stand out in these verses: jealous; revengeth; anger. God is patient, but not impotent. The Lord's POWER (vv. 3b-5). God has His way in nature. He is omnipotent. The Lord's PRESENCE (vv. 6-8). Verse 7 is one of the Bible's great verses. Everyday, whatever trials and adversities we face, we can find refuge in our ever-present God.

PRAYER: "O God, I run to You today."

NOVEMBER 20

READING: **Habakkuk 3**

" ... He will make my feet like hinds' feet ..." Habakkuk 3:19

Habakkuk deals with his problems and questions what we should do. He takes them to God. We learn in his brief book what he says (Habakkuk 1), what he sees (Habakkuk 2), and what he sings (Habakkuk 3). In his last chapter Habakkuk is a changed man. He has begun with a sob; he ends with song. He began with question marks; he ends with exclamation points. What has changed? God hadn't. His problems hadn't. The prophet changed! So he sings. A PRAYER song (vv. 1-16). His prayer needs to be our prayer today. "Lord, send a revival." God has stepped into the world in the past. He can do it now. A PRAISE song (vv. 17-19). He will have strength like a deer's feet. One day when problems end we can be on the mountaintops, jumping for joy.

PRAYER: "Lord, until today's problems are ended, I trust in You."

NOVEMBER 21

READING: Zephaniah 3

"... He will joy over thee with singing." Zephaniah 3:17

Zephaniah seems to summarize all the warnings and judgments the other prophets have given. It is a tough book! He hammers hard. Then, as so many of the prophets did, he looks beyond to a time of healing and blessing. Great times are ahead. REGATHERING (vv. 9-13). The coming Messianic Kingdom will embrace all the nations. They will have cleansed lips because they will have a cleansed heart. Jerusalem will be the center of worldwide praise to the Lord. Now Jerusalem is a source of contention. But, not when Jesus comes again! REJOICING (vv. 14-19). What a glorious picture of God is verse 17. God is saving, rejoicing and singing! Our God is a singing God. All persons of the Godhead sing: The Father (v. 17); The Son (v. 2:12); the Spirit (Ephesians 5:19).

PRAYER: "Lord, I look forward to the time when I will be in Your presence and hear You sing!"

NOVEMBER 22

READING: Haggai 2

"Consider now from this day ..." Haggai 2:18

Evidently Haggai had returned from Babylon to Jerusalem. Initially there was enthusiasm as they started the rebuilding process. But, the people got their priorities in the wrong place. They became more interested in their own houses than the Lord's house (Haggai 1:2-5). His purpose is to arouse them from their indifference and encourage them to finish rebuilding the Temple. Promised blessings didn't come. Blessing WASTED (vv. 10-14). The blessings hadn't come because they were unclean. If your life is unclean, your work will be unclean. Blessing WITHHELD (vv. 15-17). The word "consider" is the key word for Haggai (1:5,7; 2:15,18). We are to give careful thought to the reasons God's blessings have been withheld. Blessing WAITING (vv. 18-19). If we will cleanse our heart and do His work, God will bless us.

PRAYER: "Lord God, may nothing in my life hinder the blessings You have for me."

NOVEMBER 23

READING: Zechariah 6

> *"And this shall come to pass, if ye will diligently obey the voice of the Lord your God." Zechariah 6:15*

Zechariah is the prophet of visions and dreams. Four horsemen; a man with a measuring line; a flying scroll; a woman in a basket. Interested? The remnant of God's people were discouraged. Sounds a lot like today. But, Zechariah says, the future is bright. We need that encouragement, don't we? Zechariah summarizes the visions in chapter 6. CONFRONTATION (vv. 9-11). He presents the promise of a coming Priest/King. The time would come when Israel would be confronted with their true, long-rejected Messiah. CORONATION (vv. 12-13). In a beautiful service Zechariah contemplates the coronation of our Priest/King, the Lord Jesus. COMMEMORATION (vv. 14-15). People will come from far away places to worship Him! Where have you placed this King/Priest in your life?

PRAYER: "Lord Jesus, my King and Priest, I bow before You in total praise today."

NOVEMBER 24

READING: Zechariah 8

> *"... for we have heard that God is with you." Zechariah 8:23*

Much of Zechariah 8 has to do with the future and our Lord's millennial reign. There is much to learn in this future vision. REBUILDING (vv. 1-6) Jerusalem will be rebuilt and be a blessing to the world. What a beautiful picture of old men and women, back in Jerusalem, sitting on benches and telling tales. Little boys and girls will be playing in the streets. You can see this in Jerusalem today. REGATHERING (vv. 7-8). We have seen the fulfillment of Israel's restoration to their land in our day. "I will be their God" is yet to be fulfilled. REJOICING (vv. 9-19). In spite of previous problems, God promises future blessings. This brings us to the heart of true religion (vv. 16-17). REDEEMING (vv. 21-23). One day the world will see that God is among His people.

PRAYER: "Lord Jesus, today I look forward to the glorious future."

NOVEMBER 25

READING: Zechariah 11

"So they weighed for my price 30 pieces of silver." Zechariah 11:12

This section of Zechariah has been called "an incomparable treasury of prophetic truth." We see the coming (Zechariah 9), the calling (Zechariah 10) and the crucifixion of the Lord Jesus (Zechariah 11). Only Divine revelation could have given this to Zechariah. The WAILING SHEPHERDS (vv. 1-3). There will be days when false shepherds will abuse the people and lead them astray. God's people must be careful what kind of leaders they follow. The WOUNDED SHEPHERD (vv. 4-14). Zechariah symbolically assumes the role of the shepherd. He becomes a picture of the true Shepherd, the Lord Jesus. All of these events predicted were fulfilled in the rejection, betrayal and crucifixion of the Lord Jesus. The WICKED SHEPHERD (vv. 15-17). God has His Christ. Satan has his Antichrist. The world will reject God's Shepherd and receive Satan's.

PRAYER: "Lord Jesus, You are my True Shepherd. May I point people to Him."

NOVEMBER 26

READING: Zechariah 14

"In that day shall there be upon the bells of the horses, HOLINESS TO THE LORD ..." Zechariah 14:20

Much of what Zechariah predicts here is yet to be fulfilled. Prophecies about our Lord's first coming were fulfilled to the smallest detail. We can expect the same fulfillment about His second coming. These final prophecies involved Jesus and Jerusalem. We learn many things that will befall Jerusalem in the last days. RAVISHED (vv. 1-3). Things will look dark for Jerusalem as Antichrist gathers the armies of the world for the final assault upon Jerusalem. REMADE (vv. 4-15). What a thrilling picture! Jesus returns, His feet stand on the Mount of Olives and it splits like a Georgia peanut hull! King Jesus is on the scene. Battle over! RESTORED (vv. 16-21). What a glorious scene when there is holiness everywhere, even to the bridle bells of the horses!

PRAYER: "Lord Jesus, may my life ring out 'Holy to the Lord' today."

NOVEMBER 27

READING: Malachi 1

"Wherein have we despised Thy name?" Malachi 1:6

Malachi is the last book of the Old Testament. It's the "Oh really?" book. Seven times we read, "Wherein?" In Malachi's day people yawned in the face of God and said, "Oh yeah?" Through this, people showed their disrespect for God. DOUBT of God's Love (vv. 1-5). God faithfully declared His love. The people doubted it. Nothing is more heartbreaking than unreturned love. DESPISING of God's Name (v. 6). To "despise" is to show contempt for or consider worthless. If you doubt God's love, you will come to despise Him. DEFILEMENT of God's Altar (vv. 7-14). Do these verses shock you? They should. We must give to God our very best. Nothing less. To give God our leftovers is a sign of low thinking about who God is and what He has done. We must not give God the leftovers of our time, talent, or totality.

PRAYER: "Lord, today I will say to You, 'O yes'!"

NOVEMBER 28

READING: Malachi 2

"Ye have wearied the Lord with your words." Malachi 2:17

Malachi presents a series of problems God's people face today. God sets the highest standards for His people, especially those who lead God's work in any capacity. MINISTERIAL problems (vv. 1-9). Malachi appeals directly to priests who were taking advantage of their leadership position. Verses 4-7 give a picture of the marks of a true spiritual leader. MARITAL problems (vv. 10-16). God hates divorce. So does any person who has experienced its sad results. But, God does not hate those who have sorrowfully experienced divorce. MORAL problems (v. 17). It is a sad day when people are so morally confused they call evil good. Yet, God is a God of judgment and He is going to deal with moral sin. We are living in a day when people don't want to be told about judgment. But, God proves His love by His judgment against sin.

PRAYER: "Lord, these verses drive me to You today."

NOVEMBER 29

READING: **Malachi 3:1-15**

"Return unto me, and I will return unto you ... " Malachi 3:7

Our Bible promises one day Jesus will return. The COMING of the Lord (vv. 1-6). Malachi saw there would be a messenger who would announce the first coming of the Lord. John the Baptist fulfilled that role. Then, Malachi jumps the centuries and looks to our Lord's second coming. God, like a silversmith, allows us to be in the fire until He sees His own image. Refining is not to hurt us, but to help us become more like Christ. The COMMAND of the Lord (vv. 7-12). God calls us to return to Him before He returns for us (v. 7). Here we find also the much-debated verses about tithing. Don't let what is intended to be a beginning point in your giving to the Lord become a burden instead of a blessing. The COMPLAINT of the Lord (vv. 13-15).

PRAYER: "Lord, I return to You today."

NOVEMBER 30

READING: **Malachi 3:16-4:6**

"And they shall be mine ... in that day when I make up my jewels ..."
Malachi 3:17

No matter how dark and dismal the times God always has His people. Throughout his book Malachi has given attention to a smart aleck, disrespectful group. Now, attention turns to a quiet, unobtrusive remnant. God always has His faithful few. Are you in that group? If so, much awaits you. REMEMBERED (3:16). God's faithful people talk encouragingly to one another. God pricks His ear when He hears that kind of talk! He writes it all down in His "book of remembrance." RAPTURED (3:17-4:1). God's faithful people are like beautiful jewels. You are God's precious treasure. He will come for you one day! RELEASED (4:2-3). When our Savior, coming with healing wings, arrives for us we will be like young calves, released from a barn stall into the luscious spring of our Lord's presence.

PRAYER: "Even so, come, Lord Jesus!"

December

It's a Wrap!

Epistles of John, Jude and then the Revelation; quite an appropriate way to conclude a Bible. It's quite an appropriate way to wrap up the year. Let's walk together through these books of the Bible that warn about the coming apostasy and look toward the consummation of all things.

DECEMBER 1

READING: 1 John 1

"... we have fellowship one with another ..." 1 John 1:7

In his first epistle John considers our two relationships with God: sonship and fellowship. Every Christian has sonship (See John 1:12). Every Christian may have fellowship with God. The latter is conditional and can be broken. John has much to say about our fellowship with God. Its BASIS (v. 5). To have fellowship with God we must know what kind of God He is. John tells us, "God is light." And, we are told what kind of God He is not, " ... in Him is no darkness at all." To have fellowship with Him, we must walk in the light. Its BREAKING (v. 6). Our fellowship with God is broken when we "walk in darkness." Its BLESSING (v. 7). The blessing of fellowship involves walking with God and being washed in the blood of Christ, which means we claim the continual cleansing of that precious blood each day.

PRAYER: "O what fellowship, dear Lord!"

DECEMBER 2

READING: 1 John 2

"And the world passeth away ..." 1 John 2:17

To talk about a worldly Christian is like talking about a heavenly devil! But, Christians do allow themselves to be sucked in by this world system. Its MEANING (v. 15). Not the world of nature nor of humanity is intended. But, a system of things that organizes itself against God and keeps Christians from loving Him and doing His will. Its METHODS (v. 16). The world seeks to suck us into its system by appeals to the physical ("lust of the flesh"), mental ("lust of the eyes"), and spiritual ("the pride of life"). Its MASTERY (v. 17). Good news! We can overcome the world. We need to understand its passing nature. This world is in the process of passing away right now. We can choose to do the will of God. When you do you connect yourself with things eternal.

PRAYER: "O Lord, the world tempts me to things that won't last. Today, I choose things eternal."

DECEMBER 3

READING: 1 John 3

"For if our heart condemn us, God is greater than our heart ..."
1 John 3:20

Every believer in Christ may have peace of heart (See John 14:27). Yet, many face the problem of an accusing, condemning heart. We can "assure our hearts" (v. 19). ASSURANCE (vv. 19-21). Two kinds of hearts are seen here: a condemning heart and a confident one. Confidence is not found in ourselves. It is found in the greatness and knowledge of God. We assure our hearts only "before Him." ANSWERED PRAYER (vv. 22-23). We can ask God to give us assurance. Prayers are answered on the basis of His promises. If we will give a listening ear to all God commands, He will give a listening ear to what we ask Him. ABIDING (v. 24). Stay in close communion with the Lord. He will stay close to you. And assure you.

PRAYER: "Lord, I often have a condemning heart. Give me today an assured heart."

DECEMBER 4

READING 1 John 4

"God is love; and he that dwelleth in love dwelleth in God ..."
1 John 4:16

John is known as the apostle of love. God's love is the main theme of his writings. The most tremendous truth that can ever grip our heart is that God loves us. Love PROCLAIMED (vv. 7-8). John traces love to its source. God, as to His nature, is love. Love is also the nature of our family. He loves us; we love Him. Love PERSONIFIED (vv. 9-10,14). God proved He loves us by sending His Son, the Lord Jesus, into the world. When Christ became the atoning sacrifice ("propitiation") for the sins of the world (See 1 John 2:2), God's love was displayed in Him. Love PRACTICED (vv. 11-16). Now, God tells us to love one another. God's love is seen when we do.

PRAYER: "God of love, help me to show the world what You are like by my love for others."

DECEMBER 5

READING: 1 John 5

> *"... if we ask anything according to His will, He heareth us."*
> *1 John 5:14*

Prayer is crucial in the life of a believer. When we read the Bible God talks to us. When we pray we talk to God. We spend a lifetime in the school of prayer. There are no PhDs in prayer. The DIRECTION of prayer (v. 14a). We direct our prayers to God who invites us, yes, longs for us to come to Him in prayer. We come to Him in "confidence." The CONDITION of prayer (v. 14b). "Anything" is contingent upon "according to His will." Not only must we desire to know God's will. Once we discern it, we must be willing to do His will. Prayer is intended, not to get our will done in heaven, but to get God's will done on earth. The FRUITION of prayer (v. 15). When His conditions are met God promises to answer our prayers.

PRAYER: "Lord, thank You for prayer!"

DECEMBER 6

READING: 2 John

> *"... whom I love in the truth ..." 2 John 1*

What a delightful little letter to "the elect lady and her children." Either a local church and her members or a Christian lady and her children. I prefer the latter. INTRODUCTION (vv. 1-3). What a joy when a Christian lady's children are walking in the truth and living for the Lord Jesus. EXHORTATION (vv. 4-6). Truth and love are to be practiced (vv. 4-6). Isn't it strange that we must be commanded to love one another? Truth and love may be perverted (vv. 7-11). Deceivers could come and pervert truth. Don't let them in the house! Harsh? Well, it's a false love, which opens the door to false teaching. CONCLUSION (vv. 12-13). It is wonderful to visit other believers and experience joy from them.

PRAYER: "Lord, this little letter encourages me to live in truth and love and to transmit it to my children. I rejoice when they so walk."

DECEMBER 7

READING: 3 John

> *"For I rejoiced greatly, when the brethren came and testified of the truth that is in thee ..." 3 John 3*

First John was addressed to a group. Second John was sent to a woman and her family. Third John was sent to a man. Three men are introduced in this little letter. GAIUS: A COMMENDABLE Christian (v. 1-8). Gaius was a greatly loved Christian who walked in truth and was faithful to show hospitality to believers passing his way. DIOTREPHES: A CANTAKEROUS Christian (vv. 9-10). I guess all churches have one. Don't let it be you! He wanted to be first ("pre-eminence"). Only Jesus is to be first (See Colossians 1:18). Domineering, bossy church members grieve the Holy Spirit and hinder the work of the Lord. DEMETRIUS: A CONSISTENT Christian (vv. 11-14). Thank God, there was a good, godly man in the church. He had the respect of believers and non-believers as well.

PRAYER: *"Lord, help me be a Demetrius."*

DECEMBER 8

READING: Jude

> *"... earnestly contend for the faith ..." Jude 3*

Before Jesus returns the Bible teaches there will be apostasy. That is, a falling away from the faith. We read about this time in 1 Timothy 4:1ff and 2 Thessalonians 2:3ff. Those who teach apostasy we call apostates. Jude gives us a full-length portrait of the end times apostates. An EXPLANATION (vv. 1-4). Jude wanted to talk about our "common salvation," but there were apostates on the scene. The churches must be warned. An EXAMINATION (vv. 5-16). Jude gives us a past and present review of the character and conduct of apostates. The visual images from these verses are frightening and revealing. An EXHORTATION (vv. 17-25). Jude closes by giving us words of encouragement. Believers can be blessed even in the midst of apostate days. Keep on growing. Keep on praying. Keep on looking. Keep on witnessing!

PRAYER: *"Lord, I live in apostate days. Help me to be a witness in their midst."*

DECEMBER 9

READING: Revelation 1

> *"I am He that liveth, and was dead; and, behold, I am alive for*
> *evermore ..." Revelation 1:18*

The key to the Revelation is to see Jesus Christ in it. When you read difficult passages and want to get a blessing, just look for Jesus! John gives us an unveiling of the purpose and plan of the living Christ. The SETTING (vv. 9-11). John is on a lonely island. But, on the Lord's Day he was in the Spirit. Good place to be! The SECTIONS (v. 19). This 3-fold outline divides Revelation into past things (Revelation 1-3), present things (Revelation 2-3) and prospective things (Revelation 4-22). Its SUBJECT (vv. 12-18). What a glorious 7-fold description of Jesus. In the presence of such a scene John can only fall in reverence. When we see Him as the living Savior we can do nothing else.

PRAYER: "Lord Jesus, I want to see You in Your beautiful glory today."

DECEMBER 10

READING: Revelation 2

> *"Unto the angel of the church ..." Revelation 2:1*

Probably John intends the pastors of the seven churches of Asia by the word "angel" (messenger). There are several ways to study these churches. PROPHETICALLY. John seems to give us a panoramic view of the church age. From the time of the apostles to the time of the apostasy can be seen. What John saw as prophecy we now see as history. PRACTICALLY. There was a message for the actual churches existing in John's day. There is a practical message for all of our churches today. There will be a tendency for churches today to fit into one of these seven templates. PERSONALLY. At the close of each it is said, "He that hath an ear ..." Each letter has a personal message for our own heart. Look for yourself as you read these messages to the churches. God will speak to you.

PRAYER: "Lord Jesus, help me to be a Philadelphian believer, not a Laodicean one."

DECEMBER 11

READING: Revelation 3

"Him that overcometh will I make ..." Revelation 3:12

Sobering indeed are some of the messages to the seven churches. But, at the conclusion of each there is a word of exhortation to individual believers: "To him that overcometh ..." Today let's take just one; the word to Philadelphia. Look at God's three "I will" statements. Overcomers will be MADE— "I will make them a pillar ..." Not a pillow, a pillar! God promises strength, stability and solidarity. Overcomers will be MAGNIFIED— "I will write upon him ..." Overcomers will be given a 3-fold identification. Overcomers will be MARKED— "I will write ... my new name." Ah the sweet mysteries of the beauty, brilliance and blessing awaiting those who conquer through Christ.

PRAYER: "Savior, as I read about these churches, may I listen for the individual message you have for me today. I don't want to be conquered by the world, the flesh and the devil. I want to be a conqueror through Your power!"

DECEMBER 12

READING: Revelation 4

"... Come up hither ..." Revelation 4:1

Caught up to heaven John sees things that will come to pass after the church is taken away. Serious and solemn are the visions now before us. But, the central focus is of the throne of God. The word "throne" is used 12 times in Revelation 4-5. Look at the prepositions related to the "throne." ON: The PERSON on the Throne (vv. 2-3). Frightening things will take place. But, God is on His throne! ABOUT: The PEOPLE about the Throne (v. 4) The 24 elders are probably representative of the redeemed of all the ages. The saints are gathered around God's throne. BEFORE: The PRAISES before the Throne (vv. 5-11). All of the universe praises God for His glorious work of creation. What do the saints do? They "cast their crowns before the throne ..." (v. 10). Rewards for faithful service will be opportunities to fall before God in praise.

PRAYER: "O God of creation, I want something to lay at Your feet."

DECEMBER 13

READING: Revelation 5

"And they sang a new song ..." Revelation 5:9

When Jesus, the Lamb, takes the title book of the earth, heaven can no longer be silent. All heaven bursts into a celestial concert of music. Do you enjoy music? This world hears some glorious music. But, music down here is a tin whistle compared to the majesty and splendor of heaven's music. Its BASICS (v. 8). We will all sing in heaven's choir. We will have "harps," signifying praise. We will have "bowls of incense," signifying prayer. When your song is a prayer you have praise. Its LYRICS (vv. 9-10). There will be a "new song." The old song was one of creation. This "new song" will be one of redemption. And it's all built around Jesus. Its DYNAMICS (vv. 11-14). As the music swells the whole universe is lifted in song.

PRAYER: "Lord Jesus, I can hardly wait to sing to You in heaven. Help me to sing to You down here."

DECEMBER 14

READING: Revelation 6

"And I saw ... and I heard ... come and see." Revelation 6:1

The scene changes dramatically. In Revelation 4-5 we have viewed a heavenly scene. Now, the focus is upon the earth. From here to Revelation 19 unspeakable judgment will be revealed by seals, trumpets, and bowls. The description concerns the Great Tribulation (See Matthew 24:21). The action begins with seals and horses. CONQUEST (vv. 1-2). The white horse is ridden by the Antichrist who conquers with a bloodless coup. CONFLICT (vv. 3-4). The red horse represents warfare and bloodshed on the earth. CONSUMPTION (vv. 5-6). The black horse is a picture of famine and mourning. CARNAGE (vv. 7-8). The pale horse pictures death which always follows war and famine. Frightening. But, read the promise to believers (See Revelation 3:10)!

PRAYER: "Lord Jesus, thank You for Your soon return. I look forward to being caught away before Great Tribulation. May I lead many to You."

DECEMBER 15

READING: Revelation 7

"These ... came out of great tribulation, and have washed their robes ..."
Revelation 7:14

A great number who never heard about Christ will hear about Him as a result of the witness of the 144,000 (See Revelation 7:1-8). The 144,000 are Jewish evangelists who will carry the Gospel to the ends of the earth, as Jesus predicted (See Matthew 24:14). This great multitude will be Gentiles. They are called here the blood washed ones. Their DESCRIIPTION (vv. 9-12). By number, they can't be counted. By nationality, they will come from every people group on the earth. The DELIVERANCE (vv. 13-14). Picture these countless multitudes of precious people who will hear the Gospel, receive Christ, be saved and gather with us around the Throne. Their DESTINY (vv. 15-17). How wonderful to know that heaven will be a place of usefulness ("serve Him") and blessedness (vv. 16-17).

PRAYER: *"Lord Jesus, help me to lead as many to Christ as I can."*

DECEMBER 16

READING: Revelation 8

" ... and to them were given seven trumpets." Revelation 8:1

The seventh seal is opened and out tumble the seven trumpets. The same Great Tribulation period is in view. All heaven waits in suspense before the trumpet sounds, bringing intensified judgment upon the earth. The SOLEMN PREPARATION (vv. 2,6,7). Heaven's music angels make up this heavenly orchestra. Trumpets were used in the Old Testament to forecast judgment coming (See Joshua 6:1-16). The SAINTS' PRAYERS (vv. 3-5). This other angel may be Christ and the scene indicating His High Priestly work of intercession for the saints and retribution upon the earth. He takes our prayers and mingles them with His! The SINNERS' PUNISHMENTS (vv. 6-13). Now the trumpets begin to sound. One, bringing ecological disaster (v. 7). Two, bringing tragedy on the sea (vv. 8-9). Three, bringing contamination upon fresh water (vv. 10-11). Four, bringing partial darkness (v. 12).

PRAYER: *"God of heaven, I am in awe of your judgment."*

DECEMBER 17

READING: Revelation 9

"And he opened the bottomless pit ..." Revelation 9:2

This gruesome, grotesque scene gives us a glimpse into the satanic underworld. The DEVIL (v. 1). This is obviously a picture of the devil. " ... a star fall from heaven ..." reminds us that the devil is a fallen creature (See Isaiah 14; Ezekiel 28). In the Great Tribulation Satan will unleash unbelievable forces of evil upon the earth. But, keep in mind, the devil is God's devil. He can only do what God permits. The DUNGEON (v. 2). The bottomless pit is evidently a location in the satanic underworld. A penitentiary for fallen angels (See 2 Peter 2:4; Jude 6). Now, the door of separation between hell and earth is opened. The DEMONS (vv. 3-12). The locusts are demons let loose. With satanic fury they invade the earth and bring great torment. Here is the result of a choice of Satan instead of God.

PRAYER: *"Lord, I am so glad I chose Jesus."*

DECEMBER 18

READING: Revelation 10

"And I took the little book ... in my mouth sweet ... my belly was bitter" Revelation 10:10

In the midst of the tribulation passages God gives John a interlude to comfort and encourage God's people. Remember, God is still on the throne; He is in control. John did 3 things. "I saw ..." a VISION (vv. 1-3). The mighty angel John sees may very well be a vision of Christ. He holds in His hand "a little book" (v. 2). Always remember "He 's got the whole world in His hands." "I heard a VOICE ..." (vv. 4-7). Some things are concealed; other things are revealed (See Deuteronomy 29:29). Some things we wait until eternity for God to make them plain to us. "I took ..." a VOLUME (vv. 8-11). The little book points us to the Word of God. Things bitter and things sweet are found within it.

PRAYER: *"Lord Jesus, I read the Book and its message has bitter warnings and sweet blessings."*

DECEMBER 19

READING: Revelation 11

"And I will give power unto my two witnesses ..." Revelation 11:3

God always has His witnesses. The more degenerate the times, the more definite the testimonies. Two witnesses appear. They are not named. Verse 6 indicates they may be Moses and Elijah. What matters is not who they are, but what they do. Note several aspects of their ministry. The INAUGURATION (vv. 3-6). They preach a message of judgment. Surely their messages will counteract the lies of the Antichrist. The COMPLETION (vv. 7-10). They are immortal until their mission is done. And so are you! Killed by the Antichrist, their bodies will be seen worldwide. I used to wonder how this was possible. Satellite TV and worldwide internet, of course! The VINDICATION (vv. 11-12). To a startled world they will be caught up in a re-enactment of the rapture (See Revelation 4:1). The world will see what it missed.

PRAYER: "Lord, I want to be Your witness in my day."

DECEMBER 20

READING: Revelation 12

"And there appeared a great wonder in heaven; a woman ..." Revelation 12:1

Revelation 6-19 covers the Great Tribulation chronologically. Now, Revelation 12-19 gives details of major personalities. One of the most interesting is this woman. Several aspects help us understand who she is. The SYMBOLISM (vv. 1-2). The symbols of sun, moon and stars clearly point to the nation of Israel. The SORROW (vv. 3-4). The red dragon is Satan who is the source of the great sorrow the woman experiences. Satan's desire has been to devour the child of the woman. Satan has been the enemy of Jesus Christ through the centuries. The SEED (v. 5). This "man-child" is Jesus. The description fits no other. He invaded death at Calvary, died for sin, and was caught up in glorious resurrection and ascension. The SAFETY (v. 6). God supernaturally protects and provides for Israel. And He will for you!

PRAYER: "Lord, thank You that Your take care of Your own."

DECEMBER 21

READING: Revelation 13

"I ... saw a beast rise up out of the sea ..." Revelation 13:1

Beast #1 is the secular head of a revived Roman Empire. Beast #2 is the religious leader. The beast out of the sea is the Antichrist. His RISING (vv. 1-2). All the symbols indicate this beast (the Antichrist) will arise from the masses of the people in international turmoil and rebellion. He is a composite of all the dictatorial rulers of history. He has satanic-power. His RULING (vv. 3-4). He will do wonders and demand worship. His RAILING (vv. 5-8). He has a destructive mouth, and will lash out against God. In Revelation 13:9 there is a change— "He that hath an ear, let him hear." There is no mention of the churches nor the Holy Spirit (See Revelation 2:11). The church will be gone before all this takes place!

PRAYER: *"Lord, thank You that I won't be here when this happens."*

DECEMBER 22

READING: Revelation 14

" ... and with him a hundred forty and four thousand ..."
Revelation 14:1

We met the 144,000 in Revelation. They are Jewish evangelists who will preach the Gospel throughout the world (See Matthew 24:14). Now John sees them in heaven. What is said of them in heaven can be said of all believers in heaven. A HEAVENLY company (v. 1). How wonderful to know that believers are protected by the Lord. I repeat: You are immortal until your work is done. Count them. Not 143,999, but 144,000. Not a one of God's children will be lost. All will be preserved. A HAPPY company (vv. 2-3). God's people are a singing people. We sing down here. We will sing up there! And it will be a "new song," that is, superior to anything we have known before. A HOLY company (vv. 4-5). Follow the five statements true of them and of us.

PRAYER: *"Father, I look forward to being with the ransomed in glory."*

DECEMBER 23

READING: Revelation 15

"And the temple was filled with smoke from the glory of God ..."
Revelation 15:8

We are headed to the last judgments, the seven bowls of wrath. There is a lot of judgment ahead. Keep in mind that this black background makes the truth of heaven even more glorious. Revelation 15 and 16 go together. Chapter 15 gives the preliminaries of the final plagues. Chapter 16 gives the procedures of the final plagues. Two groups come into view. The MARTYRS (vv. 2-4). This group represents those who will be martyred for their faith during the Great Tribulation. They gained victory, but they went through the fire. God doesn't always deliver us from the fire. He will always deliver us through the fire. And they are singing. Evidently, there will be a lot of singing in heaven. The MESSENGERS (vv. 5-8). Heaven opens up and the angels with bowls of wrath step forth.

PRAYER: *"Father, judgment is ahead for this lost world. Help me to rescue some."*

DECEMBER 24

READING: Revelation 16

" ... pour out the vials of the wrath of God upon the earth."
Revelation 16:1

The angels proceed on their errand of doom. In rapid succession the bowls of wrath are poured out upon the earth. The CANCEROUS SORE (v. 2). A sore is an outward sign of inner corruption. The CORRUPTED SEA (v. 3). Death on the sea! The CONEMNED STREAMS (vv. 4-7). Ecological disaster. The CONTAMINATED SUN (vv 8-9). Still men won't repent. The COVERED SEAT (vv. 10-11). The attack is pressed to the very throne of Satan. The CONGREGATED SPIRITS (vv. 12-16). Satan's armies are gathered. Armageddon ahead! The CONSUMMATED STRUGGLE (vv. 17-21). And God says, "It is done." (v. 17). God's wrath is now complete. The whole universe begins to unravel. God has a message for today's world: "Flee from the wrath to come" (See Matthew 3:7).

PRAYER: *"Lord God, help me to point people to Your love so they won't experience Your wrath."*

DECEMBER 25

READING: John 3:16

"For God so loved the world ..." John 3:16

Today we turn from the frightening scenes of Revelation's judgments to the beautiful Christmas message. God's special Christmas greeting is found in this sweetest of all Christmas verses. The GOD of Christmas ("For God so loved the world ..."). Christmas reminds us that God loves the world, not just a select few. Christmas is God's way of saying to every person in the world, "I love you." The GIFT of Christmas (" ... that He gave His only begotten Son ..."). As you exchange gifts today, let each one remind you that the greatest gift of all was God giving His Son, the Lord Jesus, to die on the cross for the sins of the world (See 1 John 2:2). The GOAL of Christmas (" ... that whosoever believeth in Him, should not perish, but have everlasting life." Christmas means God has provided a way for you to be saved and spend eternity in heaven with Him.

PRAYER: "God, thank You for Your 'unspeakable gift'."

DECEMBER 26

READING: Revelation 17

" ... Mystery, Babylon the Great, the Mother of Harlots and Abominations of the Earth." Revelation 17:5

The collapse of the world church is in view under the figure of Babylon. The religious monstrosity forming before our very eyes will one day be destroyed. The Babylonian MOTHER (vv. 1-6). The true church is pictured as a pure bride. The apostate church is pictured here as a harlot. It hates God and the saints. The Babylonian MONSTER (vv. 7-11). The beast carrying the harlot church is the Roman Empire. The Babylonian MASSACRE (vv. 12-18). "Ten kings" probably refers to the leaders of the ten nations making up the Revived Roman Empire. They will battle the Lamb (v. 14) There will be insane hatred for Christ during these somber days. But, surprisingly, they will also burn the harlot (vv. 15-18). A godless civilization will use religion, then destroy it.

PRAYER: "Lord, thank You I am a part of Your precious bride, the church."

DECEMBER 27

READING: Revelation 18

"... *Come out of her, my people* ..." *Revelation 18:4*

Religious Babylon has been destroyed. Now, commercial Babylon will collapse. Here is a picture of commercialism apart from God. Civilization itself will one day fall. Several aspects of this fall are here seen. The ANNOUNCEMENT of the fall (vv. 1-8). Commercial Babylon is full of all God hates. Demons and drunkenness; lust and murder. God's call is always for His people to separate themselves (v. 4). In one day everything will come tumbling down. The ATTITUDES toward the fall (vv. 9-20). On the earth there will be great lamentation (vv. 9-19). Those who sold out to the world will mourn its passing. In heaven there will be great jubilation (v. 20). Heaven's viewpoint of things earthly is far different. The ACTUALITY of the fall (vv. 21-24). This commercial collapse will be total and complete. Only one event is left—It's time for Jesus to return to the earth!

PRAYER: *"Lord Jesus, come today!"*

DECEMBER 28

READING: Revelation 19

"*And I saw heaven opened, and behold a white horse* ..." *Revelation 19:11*

The event anticipated for centuries has now come. Jesus is returning to the earth. The ARRIVAL of the Savior (vv. 11-16). The rider of this white horse is none other than Jesus Himself. He is the "faithful and true" One. He brings His heavenly armies with Him. It's the last battle. But, hardly a battle. The war is over with a word (v. 15). The ANNOUNCEMENT of the Supper (vv. 17-18). Not the Marriage Supper. That is given in verses 7-9. This is a Supper of "flesh" being consumed. How nauseating is the flesh to God. The ANNIHILATION of Satanic Foes (vv. 19-21). The assembled armies of the Antichrist are "gathered together." But to no avail. The beast and the false prophet are thrown into the lake of fire. None will avoid God's judgment.

PRAYER: *"Lord Jesus, I am thrilled to know You again win the victory."*

DECEMBER 29

READING: Revelation 20

"And I saw a great White Throne ..." Revelation 20:11

The Great White Throne is the most awesome picture in the Bible. It is enough to sober the most frivolous heart. After the millennium and the defeat of Satan, the world will be assembled for final judgment. The SETTING (vv. 11-12). In suspended space men will gather. Today Jesus is the Savior. On that day He will be the Judge. Unbelievers will be assembled. No one will be excused nor excluded. And the books are opened. The Book of Life is also opened. None of the unbelievers at this judgment will be found in the Book of Life. The SUMMONS (v. 13). Now they will be shown they deserve the judgment that is coming to them. The SENTENCE (vv. 14-15). The second death is eternal hell. The scene is over. No description of hell. It just ends.

PRAYER: *"Lord, how awesome is this day. Thank You I settled my case out of court."*

DECEMBER 30

READING: Revelation 21

"And I saw a new heaven and a new earth ..." Revelation 21:1

Jesus said He was going away to prepare a place (See John 14:3). John takes us on a tour of our new home. Heavenly scenes thrill our heart today. Heaven's SPLENDOR (vv. 9-11). John tries to explain what he sees in human language. It breaks down. No lighting system is needed. Jesus will be the light of heaven. Heaven's STRUCTURE (vv. 12-21). Our future home, the New Jerusalem has a wall, gates, a foundation, and a street of gold. Down here men worship gold and walk on God. Up there we will worship God and walk on gold! Heaven's SAVIOR (vv. 22-27). Throughout our tour of heaven it becomes more and more apparent that Jesus is the central attraction Heaven is heaven because Jesus is there!

PRAYER: *"O Lord Jesus, You are the beauty of heaven. I look forward to the day when I see You in heaven."*

DECEMBER 31

READING: Revelation 22

" ... These sayings are faithful and true ..." Revelation 21:6

In the closing chapter of the Bible we are shown the final touches on what we can expect in heaven. Heaven has several characteristics. RETURNING (vv. 1-3a). These verses remarkably parallel Eden (See Genesis 2). There will be a beautiful river for pleasure and refreshment. There will be a bountiful tree for nourishment and healing. REJOICING (vv. 3b-4). "They shall see His face" are the five sweetest words in the Bible. What will it be when we see Christ? REIGNING (v. 5). Just think, we will reign with Christ forever and forever. We can only imagine. "How beautiful heaven must be. Sweet home of the happy and free. Fair haven of rest for the weary. How beautiful heaven must be."

PRAYER: *"Lord, You have been with me all the days of this year. I am looking forward to the time when the days of time will be ended and the ageless eons of eternity will begin."*